Freedom from the Known

从已知中解脱

[印度] 克里希那穆提 ——— 著

Sue ——— 译

九 州 出 版 社
JIUZHOUPRESS | 全国百佳图书出版单位

图书在版编目（CIP）数据

从已知中解脱 ／（印）克里希那穆提著 ；Sue译.
北京 ：九州出版社，2024. 10. -- ISBN 978-7-5225
-3499-2

Ⅰ．B945

中国国家版本馆CIP数据核字第2025WK1955号

版权合同登记号：图字 01-2022-6525
Text Copyright © 1969 Krishnamurti Foundation Trust,Ltd.
Foreword Copyright © 2010 David Skitt
Krishnamurti Foundation Trust Ltd.,
Brockwood Park, Bramdean, Hampshire, SO24 0LQ, England.
E-mail: info@kfoundation.org
Website: www.kfoundation.org
想要了解克里希那穆提的更多信息，请访问：www.jkrishnamurti.org。

从已知中解脱

作　　者	［印］克里希那穆提 著　Sue 译
责任编辑	李文君
出版发行	九州出版社
地　　址	北京市西城区阜外大街甲35号（100037）
发行电话	（010）68992190/3/5/6
网　　址	www.jiuzhoupress.com
印　　刷	鑫艺佳利（天津）印刷有限公司
开　　本	880毫米×1230毫米　32开
印　　张	8.125
字　　数	250千字
版　　次	2025年4月第1版
印　　次	2025年4月第1次印刷
书　　号	ISBN 978-7-5225-3499-2
定　　价	68.00元

This book has been written at Krishnamurti's suggestion and has his approval. The words have been chosen from a number of his recent talks (in English), taped and previously unpublished, to audiences in various parts of the world. Their selection and the order in which they are presented are my responsibility.

M.L.

本书在克里希那穆提的提议和许可下写就。书中文字选自他近期为世界各地听众所做的数篇英文讲话，这些讲话被录制了下来，但之前从未出版。这些文字的选取及其所呈现的次序由我负责。

克氏生前好友玛丽·勒琴斯女士

出版前言

克里希那穆提 1895 年生于印度，十三岁时被"通神学会"带到英国训导培养。"通神学会"由西方人士发起，以印度教和佛教经典为基础，逐步发展为一个宣扬神灵救世的世界性组织，它相信"世界导师"将再度降临，并认为克里希那穆提就是这个"世界导师"。而克里希那穆提在自己三十岁时，内心得以觉悟，否定了"通神学会"的种种谬误。1929 年，为了排除"救世主"的形象，他毅然解散专门为他设立的组织——世界明星社，宣布任何一种约束心灵解放的形式化的宗教、哲学和主张都无法带领人进入真理的国度。

克里希那穆提一生在世界各地传播他的智慧，他的思想魅力吸引了世界各地的人们，但是他坚持宣称自己不是宗教权威，拒绝别人给他加上"上师"的称号。他教导人们进行自我觉察，了解自我的局限以及宗教、民族主义狭隘性的制约。他指出打破意识束缚，进入"开放"极为重要，因为"大脑里广大的空间有着无可想象的能量"，而这个广大的空间，正是人的生命创造力的源泉所在。他提出："我只教一件事，那就是观察你自己，深入探索你自己，然后加以超越。你不是去听从我的教诲，你只是在了解自己罢了。"他的思想，为世人指明了东西方一切伟大智慧的精髓——认识自我。

克里希那穆提一生到处演讲，直到 1986 年过世，享年九十岁。他的言论、日记等被集结成六十余册著作。克里希那穆提系列作品得到了台湾著名作家胡因梦女士的倾情推荐，在此谨表谢忱。

九州出版社

译者序

　　《从已知中解脱》是克里希那穆提最为经典的一部代表作，也是最受全球读者欢迎的克氏作品之一，自 20 世纪 60 年代出版以来在全世界持续畅销。书名中的寥寥几个字——"从已知中解脱"（Freedom from the Known），精辟地概括了克里希那穆提的核心思想："人始终是过去的奴隶"，而"人的独特性就在于从他意识的内容中完全解放出来"。他认为，通过纯然的观察，摆脱过去的阴影，拥有超越时间的洞见，带来一种深刻而根本的心灵突变，达到真正的心灵自由，爱、慈悲和智慧便会不期而至，进而便可实现人与人之间真正的和谐与和平。

　　如何引发这种转变，是克里希那穆提致力于探讨的核心问题之一。这种转变并非外在的或者社会、政治、经济层面的转变，而是指内心的转变："这里说的不是外在世界的革命——不是投掷炸弹，不是浴血奋战，也不是谋反叛乱——我们必须要一起来探讨的是内在的革命"，因为克里希那穆提认为外在世界的一切问题都源于个人内心的混乱，"如果不能实现内在的、精神上的秩序，你就不可能拥有外在的秩序。危机就在这里。"而改变世界乱象的钥匙就掌握在每个人的手中——让自己的内心变得智慧清明："如果你的内在精神状态是有序的，不冲突，不矛盾，如果你的意识状态是平静、稳定、清晰的，那么你就能为这个世界带来秩序。"

　　所以，无论他与读者或听众探讨的是哪个主题，始终有一个默认的前提，那就是：如果不做特别说明，他都是从人的内心层面展开论述的，他讲的很多核心概念中都隐含了一个定语——"内在的""心理上的"。比如"时间"指的是"心理时间"，"记忆"指的是包含着内心反应或情绪感受的"心理记忆"，诸如此类不一而足，这一点读者且在阅读中慢慢体会。

Sue 2025 年于北京

C目录
CONTENTS

PART 1
第一部分

Man has throughout the ages been seeking something beyond himself, beyond material welfare—something we call truth or God or reality, a timeless state—something that cannot be disturbed by circumstances, by thought or by human corruption.

Man has always asked the question: what is it all about? Has life any meaning at all? He sees the enormous confusion of life, the brutalities, the revolt, the wars, the endless divisions of religion, ideology and nationality, and with a sense of deep abiding frustration he asks, what is one to do, what is this thing we call living, is there anything beyond it?

And not finding this nameless thing of a thousand names which he has always sought, he has cultivated faith—faith in a saviour or an ideal—and faith invariably breeds violence.

In this constant battle which we call living, we try to set a code of conduct according to the society in which we are brought up, whether it be a Communist society or a so-called free society; we accept a standard of behaviour as part of our tradition as Hindus or Muslims or Christians or whatever we happen to be. We look to someone to tell us what is right or wrong behaviour, what is right or wrong thought, and in following this pattern our conduct and our thinking become mechanical, our responses automatic. We can observe this very easily in ourselves.

For centuries we have been spoon-fed by our teachers, by our authorities, by our books, our saints. We say, "Tell me all about it—what

　　贯穿各个时代，人始终在追寻某种超越自身、超越物质福祉的存在——我们称之为真理、上帝或者真相，一种永恒的境界——追寻某种不为环境、思想或者人类的堕落所动摇的事物。

　　人们总是在问：这究竟是怎么回事？生命究竟有没有意义？目睹了生命中惊人的混乱、暴行、反叛和战争，以及宗教、意识形态和国家永无休止的分化，带着一股由来已久的深深沮丧，他问道：我们该怎么办？我们所谓"人生"到底是怎么一回事？究竟有没有什么超越之物？

　　然而，由于遍寻不获那享有千名的无名之物，人们于是培植出了信仰——对救世主或者理想的信仰——而信仰必定会衍生暴力。

　　在所谓"人生"这场经久不息的征战中，我们试图依据自身成长的社会环境——无论是共产主义社会，还是所谓自由社会——来设下一套行为规范。身为印度教徒、穆斯林、基督教徒，或是无论什么身份，我们把一套行为准则作为自身传统的一部分接受了下来。我们指望别人来告诉我们思想行为的是非对错，而在谨遵这套模式的过程中，我们的思想行为变得呆板机械，我们的反应变得自动麻木。从我们自己身上便可以轻而易举地发现这一点。

　　无数世纪以来，我们被各种导师、权威、书本和圣人用汤匙喂

lies beyond the hills and the mountains and the earth?" and we are satisfied with their descriptions, which means that we live on words and our life is shallow and empty. We are secondhand people. We have lived on what we have been told, either guided by our inclinations, our tendencies, or compelled to accept by circumstances and environment. We are the result of all kinds of influences and there is nothing new in us, nothing that we have discovered for ourselves; nothing original, pristine, clear.

Throughout theological history we have been assured by religious leaders that if we perform certain rituals, repeat certain prayers or mantras, conform to certain patterns, suppress our desires, control our thoughts, sublimate our passions, limit our appetites and refrain from sexual indulgence, we shall, after sufficient torture of the mind and body, find something beyond this little life. And that is what millions of so-called religious people have done through the ages, either in isolation, going off into the desert or into the mountains or a cave or wandering from village to village with a begging bowl, or, in a group, joining a monastery, forcing their minds to conform to an established pattern. But a tortured mind, a broken mind, a mind which wants to escape from all turmoil, which has denied the outer world and been made dull through discipline and conformity—such a mind, however long it seeks, will find only according to its own distortion.

So to discover whether there actually is or is not something beyond this anxious, guilty, fearful, competitive existence, it seems to me that one must have a completely different approach altogether. The traditional approach is from the periphery inwards, and through time, practice and renunciation, gradually to come upon that inner flower, that inner beauty and love—in fact to do everything to make oneself narrow, petty and shoddy; peel off little by little; take time; tomorrow will do, next life will

大。我们说："告诉我都是怎么回事——丘陵、群山以及大地的尽头是什么？"然后满足于他们的描述。那就意味着我们活在别人的言论中，活得肤浅而又空洞，我们都是"二手人"。我们赖以为生的，是别人告诉我们的一切，我们要么被自己的偏好和倾向所操控，要么迫于环境和际遇的压力而接受。我们是各种影响的产物，我们身上没有丝毫新东西，我们从未亲自发现过什么，没有什么是原初的、纯净的、清澈的。

贯穿整部神学史，宗教领袖们始终向我们保证：只要执行某些仪式、反复诵念某些祷文或咒语、谨遵某些模式、压制欲望、控制思想、升华激情、限制口腹之欲、克制性欲，在身心备受煎熬之后，我们便会找到某种超越这卑微人生的存在。而这正是数百万所谓宗教人士世世代代以来所做的事，要么离群索居，遁入荒漠、深山、洞穴，或是游历于村庄之间持钵行乞，要么加入某个群体，加入修道院，强迫自己的心智遵从某种既定的模式。但是一颗饱受折磨的心，一颗破碎的心，一颗只想逃避所有混乱的心，摒弃了外在世界，却又被戒律和服从磨损得迟钝不堪——这样的一颗心，即使追寻得再久，也只会找到自己扭曲之后的东西。

因此，若要发现究竟有没有某种存在，超越了这满是焦虑、愧疚、恐惧和竞争的人生，在我看来，你就必须采用一种截然不同的方式。传统的方式由周边向内探求，期望借助经年累月的修炼和克己，逐步实现内心的绽放，邂逅那份内在的美与爱。可事实上，你所做的这一切只会令自己变得狭隘、琐碎、鄙陋：由外而内一片

do—and when at last one comes to the centre one finds there is nothing there, because one's mind has been made incapable, dull and insensitive.

Having observed this process, one asks oneself, is there not a different approach altogether—that is, is it not possible to explode from the centre?

The world accepts and follows the traditional approach. The primary cause of disorder in ourselves is the seeking of reality promised by another; we mechanically follow somebody who will assure us a comfortable spiritual life. It is a most extraordinary thing that although most of us are opposed to political tyranny and dictatorship, we inwardly accept the authority, the tyranny, of another to twist our minds and our way of life. So if we completely reject, not intellectually but actually, all so-called spiritual authority, all ceremonies, rituals and dogmas, it means that we stand alone and are already in conflict with society; we cease to be respectable human beings. A respectable human being cannot possibly come near to that infinite, immeasurable, reality.

You have now started by denying something absolutely false— the traditional approach—but if you deny it as a reaction you will have created another pattern in which you will be trapped; if you tell yourself intellectually that this denial is a very good idea but do nothing about it, you cannot go any further. If you deny it however, because you understand the stupidity and immaturity of it, if you reject it with tremendous intelligence, because you are free and not frightened, you will create a great disturbance in yourself and around you but you will step out of the trap of respectability. Then you will find that you are no longer seeking. That is the first thing to learn—not to seek. When you seek you are really only window—shopping.

The question of whether or not there is a God or truth or reality, or

片剥离，花时间慢慢来，明天就可以了，来生就可以了。可是等你最后终于剥到了核心，发现那里一无所有，因为你的心早已变得无能、迟钝、麻木。

目睹了这一历程，你问自己：难道没有一种截然不同的方式吗？换句话说，难道就不能从核心爆发出来吗？

世人接受并因循着传统的方式。我们内心混乱的初始肇因，即是寻求他人所承诺的真相，我们机械地追随那些担保给我们舒适的精神生活的人。尽管我们大多数人都反对政治独裁与专制，我们内心却接受权威、专制，接受别人来扭曲我们的心灵、我们的生活方式，这真是一件极其不可思议的事。因此，如果我们全盘拒绝，并非从思想上，而是实实在在地拒绝一切所谓精神权威，一切仪轨、礼法与教条，那便意味着我们已然陷入了孤立，与社会起了冲突，我们不再是受人尊敬的体面人了。而一个所谓"体面人"，是绝无可能接近那无限的、不可估量的真相的。

现在，通过否定极端谬误的传统途径，你已经启程了。然而，如果对它的否定只是一种反应，你就已经设下了另一个禁锢自己的模式。倘若你只是从道理上告诉自己："这种否定真是个好主意"，却不付诸行动，你便无法再进一步。然而，如果你否定传统途径，是因为你懂得了它的愚蠢和幼稚，如果你以非凡的智慧摒弃了它，是因为你自由无羁、心无所惧，那么你就会在自己内心以及周遭激起巨大的不安。但你会迈出体面的陷阱，随后便会发现自己已不再追寻。这便是需要学习的第一件事——不再追寻。只要还在追寻，你实际上就只

whatever you like to call it, can never be answered by books, by priests, philosophers or saviours. Nobody and nothing can answer the question but you yourself and that is why you must know yourself. Immaturity lies only in total ignorance of self. To understand yourself is the beginning of wisdom.

And what is yourself, the individual you? I think there is a difference between the human being and the individual. The individual is a local entity, living in a particular country, belonging to a particular culture, particular society, particular religion. The human being is not a local entity. He is everywhere. If the individual merely acts in a particular corner of the vast field of life, then his action is totally unrelated to the whole. So one has to bear in mind that we are talking of the whole not the part, because in the greater the lesser is, but in the lesser the greater is not. The individual is the little conditioned, miserable, frustrated entity, satisfied with his little gods and his little traditions, whereas a human being is concerned with the total welfare, the total misery and total confusion of the world.

We human beings are what we have been for millions of years— colossally greedy, envious, aggressive, jealous, anxious and despairing, with occasional flashes of joy and affection. We are a strange mixture of hate, fear and gentleness; we are both violence and peace. There has been outward progress from the bullock cart to the jet plane but psychologically the individual has not changed at all, and the structure of society throughout the world has been created by individuals. The outward social structure is the result of the inward psychological structure of our human relationships, for the individual is the result of the total experience, knowledge and conduct of man. Each one of us is the storehouse of all the past. The individual is the human who is all mankind. The whole history of

不过是在浏览橱窗罢了。

关于是否存在上帝、真理、真相——或者无论你喜欢谓之何名——这个问题永远无法由书本、牧师、哲学家或是救世主来解答。没有任何人、任何事可以解答这个问题，除了你自己，这便是你为何必须了解自己的原因。不成熟只源于对自我的全然无知，而了解你自己正是智慧的开端。

那么你自己，身为个人的你又是什么？我认为"人"与"个人"之间是有区别的。"个人"是一个局部的存在，住在一个特定的国家里，属于某种特定的文化、特定的社会、特定的宗教。但"人"并非一个局部的存在，他无处不在。如果"个人"只在浩瀚的生命领域中一个特定的角落里行动，那么他的行动便与整体毫无干系。所以你要谨记在心，我们所谈的是整体而非局部，因为大中有小，而小中无法容大。"个人"只是一个狭隘、局限、悲惨、沮丧的存在，满足于他自己的小小神明、小小传统，而"人"关注的则是全世界整体的幸福、整体的苦难以及整体的困惑。

我们人类至今依然是数百万年来的样子——遍布惊人的贪婪、羡慕、好斗、嫉妒、焦虑以及绝望，偶尔闪现些许喜悦和关爱的火花。我们是仇恨、恐惧和温柔的奇异混合体，我们既暴力又平和。从外在讲，我们已经从牛车进步到了喷气机，但在内心里，个人依旧毫无改变，而全世界的社会结构正是由这群"个人"一手造就的。外在的社会结构是我们人际关系中内在心理结构的产物，因为个人正是人类的全部经验、知识和行为的结果。我们每个人都是储存了所有过去的仓

man is written in ourselves.

Do observe what is actually taking place within yourself and outside yourself in the competitive culture in which you live with its desire for power, position, prestige, name, success and all the rest of it—observe the achievements of which you are so proud, this whole field you call living in which there is conflict in every form of relationship, breeding hatred, antagonism, brutality and endless wars. This field, this life, is all we know, and being unable to understand the enormous battle of existence we are naturally afraid of it and find escape from it in all sorts of subtle ways. And we are frightened also of the unknown—frightened of death, frightened of what lies beyond tomorrow. So we are afraid of the known and afraid of the unknown. That is our daily life and in that there is no hope, and therefore every form of philosophy, every form of theological concept, is merely an escape from the actual reality of what is.

All outward forms of change brought about by wars, revolutions, reformations, laws and ideologies have failed completely to change the basic nature of man and therefore of society. As human beings living in this monstrously ugly world, let us ask ourselves, can this society, based on competition, brutality and fear, come to an end? Not as an intellectual conception, not as a hope, but as an actual fact, so that the mind is made fresh, new and innocent and can bring about a different world altogether? It can only happen, I think, if each one of us recognises the central fact that we, as individuals, as human beings, in whatever part of the world we happen to live or whatever culture we happen to belong to, are totally responsible for the whole state of the world.

We are each one of us responsible for every war because of the aggressiveness of our own lives, because of our nationalism, our

库，个人便是全人类，整个人类的历史就写在我们自己身上。

务请观察一下你内心和周围此刻所实际发生的一切，你所生活的这个竞争激烈的文化环境，充斥着对权力、地位、威望、名誉、成功等的欲望；仔细观察你无比自豪的各项成就，还有你所谓生活，这整片领域中的各种人际关系无不矛盾重重，催生着仇恨、对抗、残暴以及无尽的战争。我们只知道这片领地、这种人生，而因为无力看懂生活这场苦战，我们自然对它心生畏惧，寻找各种机巧的渠道来逃避它。同时，我们也害怕未知——害怕死亡，担心过了明天会怎样。因此我们既害怕已知，也害怕未知。这便是我们的日常生活，里面毫无希望，所以各种哲学、各种神学观念，都只不过是逃避现实、逃避真相的工具。

战争、革命、改革、立法以及意识形态，带来了外在形式上的各种改变，但对扭转人的本性进而改变社会本质而言，均已彻底宣告失败。身为生活在这个丑陋无比的世界上的人类，我们来问问自己：这个奠基于竞争、残暴和恐惧的社会，究竟能否终结？不是把这当作脑中的一个构想，也不是一个希望，而是一个真切的事实，这样心智才可以变得清明、新鲜而又纯真，进而造就一个截然不同的新世界。我想，唯有我们每个人都认识到这个核心事实——我们身为一群"个人"，身为人类，无论碰巧生活在世界的哪个部分，无论碰巧属于哪种文化，都对世界的整体状况负有完全的责任——才可能造就新世界。

我们每一个人对每一场战争都负有责任，因为我们个人生活中

selfishness, our gods, our prejudices, our ideals, all of which divide us. And only when we realize, not intellectually but actually, as actually as we would recognise that we are hungry or in pain, that you and I are responsible for all this existing chaos, for all the misery throughout the entire world because we have contributed to it in our daily lives and are part of this monstrous society with its wars, divisions, its ugliness, brutality and greed—only then will we act.

But what can a human being do—what can you and I do—to create a completely different society? We are asking ourselves a very serious question. Is there anything to be done at all? What can we do? Will somebody tell us? People have told us. The so-called spiritual leaders, who are supposed to understand these things better than we do, have told us by trying to twist and mould us into a new pattern, and that hasn't led us very far; sophisticated and learned men have told us and that has led us no further. We have been told that all paths lead to truth—you have your path as a Hindu and someone else has his path as a Christian and another as a Muslim, and they all meet at the same door—which is, when you look at it, so obviously absurd.

Truth has no path, and that is the beauty of truth, it is living. A dead thing has a path to it because it is static, but when you see that truth is something living, moving, which has no resting place, which is in no temple, mosque or church, which no religion, no teacher, no philosopher, nobody can lead you to—then you will also see that this living thing is what you actually are—your anger, your brutality, your violence, your despair, the agony and sorrow you live in. In the understanding of all this is the truth, and you can understand it only if you know how to look at those things in your life. And you cannot look through an ideology, through a screen of

的侵略性、我们的自私自利、我们的国家主义、我们的神明、我们的偏见和理想，这些都割裂了我们。你我对现存的一切混乱，对遍及全世界的所有苦难都负有责任，因为我们自己的日常生活就助长了这一切，我们就是这个充斥着战争、分裂、丑陋、残暴以及贪婪的可怕社会的一部分。只有当我们认识到了这一点——不是从道理上，而是真正认识到，就像我们意识到自己的饥饿或疼痛一样真切——唯有此时我们才会行动起来。

可是，要创造一个焕然一新的社会，一个人——你和我——能做些什么呢？我们正在问自己一个非常严肃的问题。究竟有什么要去做的事吗？我们能做什么？会有人来告诉我们吗？确实已经有人告诉过我们了。那些所谓"精神领袖"，貌似比我们更明白这些事情，他们试图通过扭曲和塑造我们嵌入某个新模式来教导我们，但那并没有带我们走多远。见多识广的饱学之士也教导过我们，但也没有令我们更进一步。我们总是听人说，所有道路都通往真理——你有你印度教的路，他有他基督教的路，另一个人有他穆斯林的路，他们最后都会相遇在同一道门前。倘若你仔细看一看，便会发现这个说法显然荒谬无比。

真理无路可循，而这正是真理之美，它是活生生的。只有僵死的东西才有路可循，因为它是停滞的。然而，当你发现真理是鲜活的、流动的东西，并无驻留之处，它不在任何一座寺庙、清真寺或教堂之中，也没有哪一个宗教、导师、哲学家，没有任何人能将你引向它，此时你也会发现，这鲜活的东西便是你真实的自己——你的愤怒，你

words, through hopes and fears.

So you see that you cannot depend upon anybody. There is no guide, no teacher, no authority. There is only you—your relationship with others and with the world—there is nothing else. When you realize this, it either brings great despair, from which comes cynicism and bitterness, or, in facing the fact that you and nobody else is responsible for the world and for yourself, for what you think, what you feel, how you act, all self-pity goes. Normally we thrive on blaming others, which is a form of self-pity.

Can you and I, then, bring about in ourselves without any outside influence, without any persuasion, without any fear of punishment— can we bring about in the very essence of our being a total revolution, a psychological mutation, so that we are no longer brutal, violent, competitive, anxious, fearful, greedy, envious and all the rest of the manifestations of our nature which have built up the rotten society in which we live our daily lives?

It is important to understand from the very beginning that I am not formulating any philosophy or any theological structure of ideas or theological concepts. It seems to me that all ideologies are utterly idiotic. What is important is not a philosophy of life but to observe what is actually taking place in our daily life, inwardly and outwardly. If you observe very closely what is taking place and examine it, you will see that it is based on an intellectual conception, and the intellect is not the whole field of existence; it is a fragment, and a fragment, however cleverly put together, however ancient and traditional, is still a small part of existence whereas we have to deal with the totality of life. And when we look at what is taking place in the world we begin to understand that there is no outer and inner process; there is only one unitary process, it is a whole, total movement,

的残忍，你的暴力，你的绝望，你所处的痛苦与忧伤。对这一切的领悟即是真理，而只有当你懂得了如何去看待自己生活中的这些事物，你方能领悟它。但你不能透过某种意识形态、透过文字屏障，或者透过希望与恐惧去看待它们。

于是你发现，你无法依靠任何人。没有向导，没有老师，没有权威，你只有自己——你与他人、与世界的关系——别无其他。当你认识到这一点，它要么带给你巨大的绝望，玩世不恭与愤世嫉俗接踵而至，要么你就面对这个事实：除了你，没有人为这个世界和你自己，以及你的所思、所感、所行负责——此时一切自怜都将烟消云散。我们通常热衷于归咎他人，而这正是自怜的一种表现。

那么，你和我，若不借助任何外在影响、任何劝说、任何对惩罚的恐惧，能否在自己内心，在我们存在的核心之处，引发一场彻底的革命、一场心理突变，于是我们不再残忍、暴力、争强好胜、焦虑、恐惧、贪婪、羡妒等诸如此类？——正是我们的本性显露的这些品质造就了我们日常所生活的腐败社会。

有一点很重要，从一开始就请明白：我不是在构建什么哲学或者神学的理论框架或概念。在我看来，所有的思想体系都极端愚蠢。重要的根本不是什么人生哲学，而是如实观察我们日常生活中所发生的一切，无论是内在还是外在。如果密切观察正在发生的事并仔细审视，你便会发现，它们是奠基于思想观念之上的，而思想远非生活的整个领域，思想不过是一个碎片。而一个碎片，无论构造得如何精巧，无论多么古老、多么传统，都依然只是存在极小的一部分。而我

the inner movement expressing itself as the outer and the outer reacting again on the inner. To be able to look at this seems to me all that is needed, because if we know how to look, then the whole thing becomes very clear, and to look needs no philosophy, no teacher. Nobody need tell you how to look. You just look.

Can you then, seeing this whole picture, seeing it not verbally but actually, can you easily, spontaneously, transform yourself? That is the real issue. Is it possible to bring about a complete revolution in the psyche?

I wonder what your reaction is to such a question? You may say, "I don't want to change", and most people don't, especially those who are fairly secure socially and economically or who hold dogmatic beliefs and are content to accept themselves and things as they are or in a slightly modified form. With those people we are not concerned. Or you may say more subtly, "Well, it's too difficult, it's not for me", in which case you will have already blocked yourself, you will have ceased to enquire and it will be no use going any further. Or else you may say, "I see the necessity for a fundamental inward change in myself but how am I to bring it about? Please show me the way, help me towards it."If you say that, then what you are concerned with is not change itself; you are not really interested in a fundamental revolution: you are merely searching for a method, a system, to bring about change.

If I were foolish enough to give you a system and if you were foolish enough to follow it, you would merely be copying, imitating, conforming, accepting, and when you do that you have set up in yourself the authority of another and hence there is conflict between you and that authority. You feel you must do such and such a thing because you have been told to do it and yet you are incapable of doing it. You have your own particular

们所面对的，是人生的整体。同时，当我们观察世上所发生的事，我们就会开始懂得：只存在一个一体的进程，并无内外之分，它是一场整体的、统一的运动——内在的活动从外在表现出来，同时外在又对内在做出反应。能够看到这一点，在我看来已经足够，因为，如果我们懂得如何去看，那么所有事情都会变得非常清晰。而"看"并不需要哲学和导师，没人需要告诉你如何去看，你只要看就好。

那么，看到了这整幅图景——不是口头上明白，而是真正地看到——你能否轻松自在地转变自己？这才是真正的问题所在。有没有可能引发一场彻底的心灵革命？

我想知道对于这样一个问题，你会做何反应？你也许会说："我不想改变。"大部分人也确实如此，尤其是那些具有相当牢靠的经济与社会地位的人，那些信守教条、接受并满足自身现状或是愿意稍做改良的人。那些人不是我们关注的对象。或者，你也许会更委婉地陈词："哦，那太难了，不适合我。"这样的话，你就已经阻碍了自己，你就已经停止了探询，再说下去也就没什么意义了。又或者，你也许会说："我明白自己内心彻底转变的必要性，但要如何才能实现呢？请为我指明出路，帮我向前迈进！"如果你这么说，那么你关心的并非转变本身，你对彻底的革命并非真的感兴趣，你只不过在寻找引发改变的一个方法、一套体系罢了。

如果我蠢到要给你一套体系，如果你也蠢到会遵奉这套体系，那么你就只是在照搬、模仿、遵从、接受。倘若你这么做，你就已经在自己内心将他人奉为权威，你与权威之间便有了冲突。你觉得自己必

inclinations, tendencies and pressures which conflict with the system you think you ought to follow and therefore there is a contradiction. So you will lead a double life between the ideology of the system and the actuality of your daily existence. In trying to conform to the ideology, you suppress yourself—whereas what is actually true is not the ideology but what you are. If you try to study yourself according to another you will always remain a secondhand human being.

A man who says, "I want to change, tell me how to", seems very earnest, very serious, but he is not. He wants an authority whom he hopes will bring about order in himself. But can authority ever bring about inward order? Order imposed from without must always breed disorder. You may see the truth of this intellectually but can you actually apply it so that your mind no longer projects any authority, the authority of a book, a teacher, a wife or husband, a parent, a friend or of society? Because we have always functioned within the pattern of a formula, the formula becomes the ideology and the authority; but the moment you really see that the question, "How can I change?" sets up a new authority, you have finished with authority for ever.

Let us state it again clearly: I see that I must change completely from the roots of my being; I can no longer depend on any tradition because tradition has brought about this colossal laziness, acceptance and obedience; I cannot possibly look to another to help me to change, not to any teacher, any God, any belief, any system, any outside pressure or influence. What then takes place?

First of all, can you reject all authority? If you can it means that you are no longer afraid. Then what happens? When you reject something false which you have been carrying about with you for generations, when you

须如此这般，因为别人告诉你要这么做，可你就是做不到。你有自己特定的个性、倾向以及压力，这些与你认为理应遵从的体系相冲突，矛盾于是接踵而至。因此，你在理论体系与实际日常生活的夹缝中，过着一种双重生活。为了谨遵那套观念，你压抑自己，可实际上真实的并非观念，而是你实际的样子。只要你试图参照他人来了解自己，那么你就永远只能做一个"二手货"。

倘若一个人说："我希望改变，告诉我怎么做"，尽管他看起来非常诚恳、非常认真，但事实并非如此。他希望有个权威能为他营造内心的秩序，可是权威到底能带来内心的秩序吗？外在强加的秩序不可避免地会催生失序。你也许从道理上明白了这个真相，但是你能真正加以实施吗？那样的话，你的心就不会再投射任何权威——书本、导师、妻子或丈夫、父母、朋友或社会的权威。因为我们一直在模式的框架内生活，模式就变成了观念和权威。然而，一旦你真的看穿，"我如何才能改变"这个问题树立了一个新的权威，你便一劳永逸地了结了所有权威。

我们再来清楚地重申一下：我发现我必须从自身存在的根本处彻底转变；我不能再仰仗任何传统，因为传统造成了这可怕的懒散、接受与服从；我也不可能指望别人来帮我改变，包括任何老师、任何上帝、任何信仰、任何体系、任何外来的压力或者影响。然后会怎么样？

首先，你能否摒弃所有权威？如果可以，那就意味着你已不再恐惧。然后会怎么样？当你摒弃了世世代代以来所背负的谬误，当你抛

throw off a burden of any kind, what takes place? You have more energy, haven't you? You have more capacity, more drive, greater intensity and vitality. If you do not feel this, then you have not thrown off the burden, you have not discarded the dead weight of authority.

But when you have thrown it off and have this energy in which there is no fear at all—no fear of making a mistake, no fear of doing right or wrong —then is not that energy itself the mutation? We need a tremendous amount of energy and we dissipate it through fear but when there is this energy which comes from throwing off every form of fear, that energy itself produces the radical inward revolution. You do not have to do a thing about it.

So you are left with yourself, and that is the actual state for a man to be who is very serious about all this; and as you are no longer looking to anybody or anything for help, you are already free to discover. And when there is freedom, there is energy; and when there is freedom it can never do anything wrong. Freedom is entirely different from revolt. There is no such thing as doing right or wrong when there is freedom. You are free and from that centre you act. And hence there is no fear, and a mind that has no fear is capable of great love. And when there is love it can do what it will.

What we are now going to do, therefore, is to learn about ourselves, not according to me or to some analyst or philosopher—because if we learn about ourselves according to someone else, we learn about them, not ourselves—we are going to learn what we actually are.

Having realized that we can depend on no outside authority in bringing about a total revolution within the structure of our own psyche, there is the immensely greater difficulty of rejecting our own inward authority, the authority of our own particular little experiences and accumulated opinions, knowledge, ideas and ideals. You had an experience

下了所有负担，会发生什么？你就拥有了更多的能量，不是吗？你有了更多的能力、动力、热情以及活力。如果没有这样的感受，那么你就还没有抛下包袱，你尚未摒弃权威的僵死重负。

然而，一旦你将它抛下，拥有了这股无所畏惧的能量——不害怕犯错，不担心做对还是做错——你那股能量本身不就是突变吗？我们需要无穷的能量，之前我们因为恐惧而耗费了它。可是，一旦抛下所有恐惧因而拥有了活力，那股活力本身便会带来内心的彻底革命，你什么都不必做。

于是你就只剩下自己了，而对这些问题非常认真的人，实际上便会处于这样的状态。由于你不再指望任何人、任何事来帮你，你便已然具备了探索的自由。一旦有了自由，也就有了活力；一旦有了自由，就永远不会做错。但自由与反叛有着天壤之别。一旦有了自由，就根本没有做对还是做错这回事。你是自由的，你便会从那个核心出发去行动，因此心无所惧。一颗无惧的心是有能力付出大爱的，有了这样的爱，便可以从心所欲了。

因此，我们此刻要做的，就是了解自己，但不能按照我或者某个分析师、某个哲学家的说法去了解。因为如果参照别人来了解自己，我们了解的就是他们，而不是我们自己了——我们要了解的是自己的真相。

我们已经认识到无法仰仗外在的权威，来引发我们自身心智结构的彻底革命。此时我们面临着一个更为严峻的挑战：摒弃我们自己内在的权威——我们自身特定的琐碎经验，以及累积的观点、知识、理

yesterday which taught you something and what it taught you becomes a new authority—and that authority of yesterday is as destructive as the authority of a thousand years. To understand ourselves needs no authority either of yesterday or of a thousand years because we are living things, always moving, flowing, never resting. When we look at ourselves with the dead authority of yesterday, we will fail to understand the living movement and the beauty and quality of that movement.

To be free of all authority, of your own and that of another, is to die to everything of yesterday, so that your mind is always fresh, always young, innocent, full of vigour and passion. It is only in that state that one learns and observes. And for this a great deal of awareness is required, actual awareness of what is going on inside yourself, without correcting it or telling it what it should or should not be, because the moment you correct it you have established another authority, a censor.

So now we are going to investigate ourselves together—not one person explaining while you read, agreeing or disagreeing with him as you follow the words on the page, but taking a journey together, a journey of discovery into the most secret corners of our minds. And to take such a journey we must travel light; we cannot be burdened with opinions, prejudices and conclusions—all that old furniture we have collected for the last two thousand years and more. Forget all you know about yourself; forget all you have ever thought about yourself; we are going to start as if we knew nothing.

It rained last night heavily, and now the skies are beginning to clear; it is a new fresh day. Let us meet that fresh day as if it were the only day. Let us start on our journey together with all the remembrance of yesterday left behind—and begin to understand ourselves for the first time.

念和理想。你昨天有了一次经验，教了你一些东西，它所教你的，变成了新的权威，而昨天的这种权威跟数千年来的权威具有同等的破坏性。要了解自我，既不需要昨天的，也不需要数千年来的权威，因为我们是鲜活的、动态的存在，始终流动着，从不停歇。一旦用昨日的僵死权威来看自己，我们就无法理解这鲜活的动态，无法领会那场运动的美与品质。

若要摆脱所有的权威——自己与他人的权威——就要对昨日的一切死去，这样你的心就始终是新鲜、年轻、纯真的，洋溢着活力与激情。唯有在这样的心境中，你才能学习和观察。为此需要极高的觉知力，如实觉知自己内心发生的一切，既不纠正也不评判应当不应当，因为一旦去纠正，你便树立了另一个权威，一个审查者。

因此，我们现在要一起来探查自我。这并非你阅读时有个人从旁解释，你一边跟随书页上的文字，一边表示同意或不同意，而是我们并肩踏上一段旅程，一段深入我们内心最神秘角落的探索之旅。若要踏上这段旅程，我们就必须轻装上路，不能背负着观点、成见和结论——我们两千多年搜罗来的所有旧家具。忘掉你关于自己所知的一切，忘掉你对自己的所有想法，我们要一无所知地启程。

昨夜豪雨如注，而此刻的天空已开始放晴，崭新的一天开始了。让我们迎接这新的一天，就如同它是此生仅有的一天。让我们一起踏上征程，把昨日的记忆抛诸脑后，重新开始了解自己，宛若初见。

PART 2
第二部分

If you think it is important to know about yourself only because I or someone else has told you it is important, then I am afraid all communication between us comes to an end. But if we agree that it is vital that we understand ourselves completely, then you and I have quite a different relationship, then we can explore together with a happy, careful and intelligent enquiry.

I do not demand your faith; I am not setting myself up as an authority. I have nothing to teach you—no new philosophy, no new system, no new path to reality; there is no path to reality any more than to truth. All authority of any kind, especially in the field of thought and understanding, is the most destructive, evil thing. Leaders destroy the followers and followers destroy the leaders. You have to be your own teacher and your own disciple. You have to question everything that man has accepted as valuable, as necessary.

If you do not follow somebody you feel very lonely. Be lonely then. Why are you frightened of being alone? Because you are faced with yourself as you are and you find that you are empty, dull, stupid, ugly, guilty and anxious—a petty, shoddy, secondhand entity. Face the fact; look at it, do not run away from it. The moment you run away fear begins.

In enquiring into ourselves we are not isolating ourselves from the rest of the world. It is not an unhealthy process. Man throughout the world is caught up in the same daily problems as ourselves, so in enquiring

如果你认为自我了解很重要，只是因为我或者其他人告诉你这很重要，那么恐怕我们之间的交流便到此为止了。然而，如果我们都同意：彻底了解自我是件生死攸关的事，那么你我就有了一份截然不同的关系。然后我们便可以带着一份愉悦、仔细而又睿智的探询之心，一起去探索了。

我不要求你相信我，我也不会自封权威。我没什么要传授给你的——没有通往真相的新哲学、新体系、新途径；正如真理无路可循，真相亦无路可循。任何形式的权威，尤其是思想与领悟方面的，是最具破坏性、最邪恶的东西。领袖毁掉了追随者，追随者也毁掉了领袖。你必须成为自己的导师和自己的弟子，你必须质疑人们公认有价值、有必要的一切。

如果不追随某个人你会觉得非常孤单，那么就孤单好了！你为何害怕孤单？因为当你如实面对自己，你会发现自己空洞、迟钝、愚蠢、丑陋、愧疚、焦虑，是一个琐碎卑微的二手货。面对这个事实，看着它，不要逃避；你一逃避，恐惧便出现了。

探究自我，并不是将我们自己与世界隔绝开来，这不是一个病态的过程。全世界的人都跟我们一样，把自己困在了同样的日常问题当中，所以说探索自我丝毫不会令我们变得神经质，因为个人与集体并

into ourselves we are not being in the least neurotic because there is no difference between the individual and the collective. That is an actual fact. I have created the world as I am. So don't let us get lost in this battle between the part and the whole.

I must become aware of the total field of my own self, which is the consciousness of the individual and of society. It is only then, when the mind goes beyond this individual and social consciousness, that I can become a light to myself that never goes out.

Now where do we begin to understand ourselves? Here am I, and how am I to study myself, observe myself, see what is actually taking place inside myself? I can observe myself only in relationship because all life is relationship. It is no use sitting in a corner meditating about myself. I cannot exist by myself. I exist only in relationship to people, things and ideas, and in studying my relationship to outward things and people, as well as to inward things, I begin to understand myself. Every other form of understanding is merely an abstraction and I cannot study myself in abstraction; I am not an abstract entity; therefore I have to study myself in actuality—as I am, not as I wish to be.

Understanding is not an intellectual process. Accumulating knowledge about yourself and learning about yourself are two different things, for the knowledge you accumulate about yourself is always of the past and a mind that is burdened with the past is a sorrowful mind. Learning about yourself is not like learning a language or a technology or a science—then you obviously have to accumulate and remember; it would be absurd to begin all over again—but in the psychological field learning about yourself is always in the present and knowledge is always in the past, and as most of us live in the past and are satisfied with the past, knowledge becomes extraordinarily

无分别。这是一个千真万确的事实：我依照自己的样子创造了这个世界。因此我们不要迷失在这场局部与整体的争论中。

我必须充分觉知自我的整个版图，也就是个人与社会的意识。唯有当心灵超越了个人与社会的意识，我才能成为照亮自己、永不熄灭的明灯。

那么，我们要从何处开始了解自己呢？我就在这里，我要如何探究自己、观察自己，看清自己内心实际发生的事呢？我只能在关系中观察自己，因为生活全部都是关系。坐在角落里冥想自我，这么做毫无意义。我无法孤立存在，我只能活在与他人、事物及概念的关系当中。通过探究我与外在的人事物以及与内心活动的关系，我便开始了自我了解。其他任何形式的了解都不过是抽象思考而已，而我无法通过抽象思考来探究自我。我并非一个抽象的存在，因此我必须在现实中探究自我，如我所是，而非如我所愿。

了解并非一个智力过程。积累关于自己的知识与了解自己是两码事，因为你积累的关于自己的知识始终属于过去，而一颗为过去所负累的心，是一颗哀伤的心。了解自己不像学习一门语言、一门技术或科学——那时你显然必须积累以及铭记，凡事都从头来过就太荒唐了。但在心理领域，了解自己始终是一件当下的事，而知识则永远属于过去。由于我们大多数人都活在过去、满足于过去，知识对我们才变得至关重要，我们也因此而崇拜博学、聪明、慧黠的人。但是，如果你时时刻刻、每分每秒都在学习，通过观察和倾听，通过看和做来学习，那么你就会发现，学习是一场恒常的运动，丝毫没有过去。

important to us. That is why we worship the erudite, the clever, the cunning. But if you are learning all the time, learning every minute, learning by watching and listening, learning by seeing and doing, then you will find that learning is a constant movement without the past.

If you say you will learn gradually about yourself, adding more and more, little by little, you are not studying yourself now as you are but through acquired knowledge. Learning implies a great sensitivity. There is no sensitivity if there is an idea, which is of the past, dominating the present. Then the mind is no longer quick, pliable, alert. Most of us are not sensitive even physically. We overeat, we do not bother about the right diet, we oversmoke and drink so that our bodies become gross and insensitive; the quality of attention in the organism itself is made dull. How can there be a very alert, sensitive, clear mind if the organism itself is dull and heavy? We may be sensitive about certain things that touch us personally but to be completely sensitive to all the implications of life demand that there be no separation between the organism and the psyche. It is a total movement.

To understand anything you must live with it, you must observe it, you must know all its content, its nature, its structure, its movement. Have you ever tried living with yourself? If so, you will begin to see that yourself is not a static state, it is a fresh living thing. And to live with a living thing your mind must also be alive. And it cannot be alive if it is caught in opinions, judgements and values.

In order to observe the movement of your own mind and heart, of your whole being, you must have a free mind, not a mind that agrees and disagrees, taking sides in an argument, disputing over mere words, but rather following with an intention to understand—a very difficult thing to do because most of us don't know how to look at, or listen to, our own

如果你说你要慢慢了解自己，一点一滴地累积，你便不是在如实地探究此刻的自己，而是借助以前获取的知识。了解之中包含着高度的敏感性。然而，只要有个过去的观念主宰着现在，敏感性就不复存在了，进而你的心也不再迅捷、柔韧、警觉。我们大多数人连身体都不敏感，我们饮食过量，不注重合理的膳食，我们烟酒过度，身体因而变得臃肿麻木，有机体本身的注意力受损下降。倘若连身体都迟钝沉重，又怎么可能拥有一颗警觉、敏锐、清明的心呢？我们也许对某些触动我们个人的事很敏感，但是若要对生命所包含的一切都全然敏感，就需要身体与心灵融合无间，因为那是一个整体的进程。

若要了解什么，你就必须与它共存，你就必须观察它，探明它的全部内容、本质、结构以及活动。你可曾试过与自己共处？如果你试过，便会发现你自己并不是静态的，而是一个新鲜的、活生生的存在。若要与一个活物共处，你的心就必须同样鲜活。倘若被困在了观点、评判与价值观当中，它是无法鲜活起来的。

若要观察你自己的头脑和内心、你整个生命的活动，你就必须拥有一颗自由的心，不是一颗表示同意不同意、在争论中站边、只热衷文字辩论的心，而是带着了解的意愿时刻去跟随的心。这实在很难做到，因为我们大多数人都不知道如何去观察、去倾听自己的生命，就像我们不懂得如何观赏江河之美，也不懂得如何倾听树间的微风。

我们一旦谴责或是辩护，就无法看清真相；当我们的心一直喋喋不休，我们也无法看清真相。此时我们不再观察事实，而只是盯着自己造出的投影。我们每个人都抱有自我形象，认为自己如何或应当如

being any more than we know how to look at the beauty of a river or listen to the breeze among the trees.

When we condemn or justify we cannot see clearly, nor can we when our minds are endlessly chattering; then we do not observe what is; we look only at the projections we have made of ourselves. Each of us has an image of what we think we are or what we should be, and that image, that picture, entirely prevents us from seeing ourselves as we actually are.

It is one of the most difficult things in the world to look at anything simply. Because our minds are very complex we have lost the quality of simplicity. I don't mean simplicity in clothes or food, wearing only a loin cloth or breaking a record fasting or any of that immature nonsense the saints cultivate, but the simplicity that can look directly at things without fear—that can look at ourselves as we actually are without any distortion—to say when we lie we lie, not cover it up or run away from it.

Also in order to understand ourselves we need a great deal of humility. If you start by saying,"I know myself", you have already stopped learning about yourself; or if you say, "There is nothing much to learn about myself because I am just a bundle of memories, ideas, experiences and traditions", then you have also stopped learning about yourself. The moment you have achieved anything you cease to have that quality of innocence and humility; the moment you have a conclusion or start examining from knowledge, you are finished, for then you are translating every living thing in terms of the old. Whereas if you have no foothold, if there is no certainty, no achievement, there is freedom to look, to achieve. And when you look with freedom it is always new. A confident man is a dead human being.

But how can we be free to look and learn when our minds from the moment we are born to the moment we die are shaped by a particular

何，正是那个形象、那幅图景，彻底妨碍了我们如实地看到自己。

世上最难的事之一，就是去简单地看待事情。因为我们的心太过复杂，我们已然失去了简单的品质。我所说的"简单"，并非圣人们所教化的衣食节俭，只裹一块腰布，打破断食纪录，以及任何不成熟的类似愚行，而是心无所惧、直截了当地看待事物——这样一种简单。换言之，就是能够如其所是、毫无扭曲地看待我们自己，说谎时即承认说谎，不掩饰，也不逃避。

同时，若要了解自己，我们也需要极为谦卑。如果你一开始就说："我懂我自己"，你就已经停止了自我了解；抑或你说，"关于自我没什么可了解的，因为我不过是一团记忆、观点、经验与传统罢了"，那样你也停止了自我了解。你一旦获得了什么，便不再具备单纯与谦卑的品质；你一旦得出结论或者开始用知识去探查，你就完蛋了，因为此时你就是在按照老一套来诠释每一样活生生的事物。然而，倘若你没有立足点，不确信什么，也不抱持过往所得，你便有了去看、去达成的自由。当你能够自由地去看，一切都是崭新的。一个过分自信的人，就如同死人一般。

然而，从生到死，我们的心一直被某种特定的文化，用"自我"这个狭隘的模式塑造着，我们又怎能自由地去看、去了解？数个世纪以来，我们一直受制于国籍、等级、阶层、传统、宗教、语言、教育、文学、艺术、习俗、陈规，受制于各种舆论和经济压力，受制于我们所吃的食物、所处的气候，受制于我们的家庭、我们的朋友、我们的经验——你所能想到的各种影响——因此我们对每个问题的反应

culture in the narrow pattern of the"me"? For centuries we have been conditioned by nationality, caste, class, tradition, religion, language, education, literature, art, custom, convention, propaganda of all kinds, economic pressure, the food we eat, the climate we live in, our family, our friends, our experiences—every influence you can think of—and therefore our responses to every problem are conditioned.

Are you aware that you are conditioned? That is the first thing to ask yourself, not how to be free of your conditioning. You may never be free of it, and if you say, "I must be free of it", you may fall into another trap of another form of conditioning. So are you aware that you are conditioned? Do you know that even when you look at a tree and say, "That is an oak tree", or "that is a banyan tree", the naming of the tree, which is botanical knowledge, has so conditioned your mind that the word comes between you and actually seeing the tree? To come in contact with the tree you have to put your hand on it and the word will not help you to touch it.

How do you know you are conditioned? What tells you? What tells you you are hungry? —not as a theory but the actual fact of hunger? In the same way, how do you discover the actual fact that you are conditioned? Isn't it by your reaction to a problem, a challenge? You respond to every challenge according to your conditioning and your conditioning being inadequate will always react inadequately.

When you become aware of it, does this conditioning of race, religion and culture bring a sense of imprisonment? Take only one form of conditioning, nationality, become seriously, completely aware of it and see whether you enjoy it or rebel against it, and if you rebel against it, whether you want to break through all conditioning. If you are satisfied with your conditioning you will obviously do nothing about it, but if you are not

都受到了制约。

你有没有发觉自己深受制约？这才是你首先要问自己的，而不是如何摆脱制约。你或许从未摆脱它，但是倘若你说："我必须摆脱它"，你便落入了另一种形式的制约所设下的另一个陷阱。所以要问，你有没有发觉自己深受制约？你知不知道，哪怕是你看着一棵树说："这是一棵橡树"或"那是一棵榕树"——叫出树的名字，本属于植物学知识——可那也已经深深地制约了你的头脑，乃至名词挡住了你真正去看那棵树？要想接触那棵树，你就得把手放在上面，而词语是不会帮你去触摸它的。

你如何才能知道你受到了制约？什么能告诉你这点？是什么告诉你"你饿了"——不是假设，而是你真的饿了？同样，你如何发现"你深受制约"这个真切的事实？难道不是通过你对问题或是挑战的反应吗？你对每个挑战所做的反应，都来源于你所受的制约，而由于你受到了不恰当的制约，你的反应始终都是不恰当的。

当你开始意识到这一点，种族、宗教、文化的这些制约，是不是带给你一种被囚禁的感觉？我们仅以一种制约形式为例——国籍，我们来认真地、彻底地认清它，看看你究竟对它是欣赏还是反对；倘若你反对，你又是否愿意打破一切制约。如果你满意自己所受的制约，你显然不会动它丝毫；但是，如果你不满意，当你开始察觉到它，你便会发现自己所做的一切从未摆脱它的影响。从未！所以说你一直与已死之物一起活在过去。

只有当你在延续快乐、逃避痛苦时遇到了冲突，你才能亲自发

satisfied when you become aware of it, you will realize that you never do anything without it. Never! And therefore you are always living in the past with the dead.

You will be able to see for yourself how you are conditioned only when there is a conflict in the continuity of pleasure or the avoidance of pain. If everything is perfectly happy around you, your wife loves you, you love her, you have a nice house, nice children and plenty of money, then you are not aware of your conditioning at all. But when there is a disturbance—when your wife looks at someone else or you lose your money or are threatened with war or any other pain or anxiety—then you know you are conditioned. When you struggle against any kind of disturbance or defend yourself against any outer or inner threat, then you know you are conditioned. And as most of us are disturbed most of the time, either superficially or deeply, that very disturbance indicates that we are conditioned. So long as the animal is petted he reacts nicely, but the moment he is antagonized the whole violence of his nature comes out.

We are disturbed about life, politics, the economic situation, the horror, the brutality, the sorrow in the world as well as in ourselves, and from that we realize how terribly narrowly conditioned we are. And what shall we do? Accept that disturbance and live with it as most of us do? Get used to it as one gets used to living with a backache? Put up with it?

There is a tendency in all of us to put up with things, to get used to them, to blame them on circumstances. "Ah, if things were right I would be different", we say, or, "Give me the opportunity and I will fulfil myself", or, "I am crushed by the injustice of it all", always blaming our disturbances on others or on our environment or on the economic situation.

If one gets used to disturbance it means that one's mind has become dull,

现你受到了制约。如果你周围的一切都无比幸福，妻子爱你，你也爱她，你们有座漂亮的房子，有乖巧的孩子和丰厚的财产，你根本就不会发觉自己的局限。但是，当生活中出现了干扰——你妻子看上了别人，你损失了财产，受到了战争或是其他痛苦、焦虑的威胁——然后你就知道自己是受限的了。当你奋力抗争各种干扰，或是保护自己免遭各种内忧外患，你便会发现自己深受局限。由于我们大部分人多数时候都在遭受侵扰，无论层次深浅，那些侵扰本身便说明了我们的局限。那就像是，只要一个动物得到爱抚，它就会友善地回应，可是一旦被惹恼，它本性中的所有暴力就全部爆发了出来。

我们受到了各种侵扰：生活、政治与经济局势，世界上以及我们内心的恐怖、残暴、悲伤，从这里便能看出我们所受的局限是多么严重、多么狭隘。那我们该怎么办？接受那些侵扰然后得过且过，就像大多数人那样吗？对它习以为常，就像你习惯了背痛那样？或者忍受下去？

我们身上都有一种对事情逆来顺受、习以为常、归咎于环境的倾向。我们说："啊，如果情况顺利我就会不一样"，或者，"只要给我机会，我便能成就自己"，又或者，"我是因为遭受了不公正的待遇才垮掉的"，我们总是把自己遭受的干扰归咎于他人、环境或是经济形势。

如果一个人对干扰习以为常，那就说明他的心已然变得迟钝，就像是看惯了周遭的美景，从此视而不见。他变得冷漠、僵硬、无情，他的心也变得越来越迟钝。如果我们不习惯，便会想方设法逃避：服

just as one can get so used to beauty around one that one no longer notices it. One gets indifferent, hard and callous, and one's mind becomes duller and duller. If we do not get used to it we try to escape from it by taking some kind of drug, joining a political group, shouting, writing, going to a football match or to a temple or church or finding some other form of amusement.

Why is it that we escape from actual facts? We are afraid of death—I am just taking that as an example—and we invent all kinds of theories, hopes, beliefs, to disguise the fact of death, but the fact is still there. To understand a fact we must look at it, not run away from it. Most of us are afraid of living as well as of dying. We are afraid for our family, afraid of public opinion, of losing our job, our security, and hundreds of other things. The simple fact is that we are afraid, not that we are afraid of this or that. Now why cannot we face that fact?

You can face a fact only in the present and if you never allow it to be present because you are always escaping from it, you can never face it, and because we have cultivated a whole network of escapes we are caught in the habit of escape.

Now, if you are at all sensitive, at all serious, you will not only be aware of your conditioning but you will also be aware of the dangers it results in, what brutality and hatred it leads to. Why, then, if you see the danger of your conditioning, don't you act? Is it because you are lazy, laziness being lack of energy? Yet you will not lack energy if you see an immediate physical danger like a snake in your path, or a precipice, or a fire. Why, then, don't you act when you see the danger of your conditioning? If you saw the danger of nationalism to your own security, wouldn't you act?

The answer is you don't see. Through an intellectual process of analysis you may see that nationalism leads to self-destruction but there is

用药物、加入政治团体、呐喊、写作，看足球赛，造访寺庙或教堂，或是寻找其他形式的娱乐。

我们究竟为何逃避事实？我们恐惧死亡——我只是以此为例——于是发明出各种理论、希望、信仰来掩盖死亡这一事实，但它依然在那里。要了解一个事实，我们就必须正视它，不逃避。我们大多数人既恐惧生活，也恐惧死亡。我们担忧家人，惧怕公众舆论，害怕丢掉工作，担心保障问题，以及数不清的其他事情。一个再简单不过的事实便是：我们心存恐惧，而不是我们怕这还是怕那。可我们为什么就是不能直面这一事实呢？

你只能在当下面对事实。如果你因为一直在逃避而从不允许它在当下呈现，你便永远无法面对它。而由于我们已经培植了一整套逃避的网络，我们深深陷在了逃避的陋习当中。

然而，如果你真的敏感认真，那么你不仅会发觉自己的局限，也会发觉它招来的危险，它导致的残暴和仇恨。接下来，如果看到了局限的危险，你又为何不行动？是因为你懒惰，因为缺乏活力吗？可是，如果看到身体上有个迫在眉睫的危险，比如，挡在路上的一条蛇，或是一座悬崖、一团火，你是不会没有活力的。那么，当你看到了局限的危险，你为何不行动呢？如果你看到了国家主义对你自身安全的威胁，你为何没有行动？

答案是你并没有看到。借助智力上的分析过程，你或许能理解国家主义会导致自我毁灭，但那份理解当中没有充沛的情感。唯有当内心情感充沛时，你才会变得活力四射。

no emotional content in that. Only when there is an emotional content do you become vital.

If you see the danger of your conditioning merely as an intellectual concept, you will never do anything about it. In seeing a danger as a mere idea there is conflict between the idea and action and that conflict takes away your energy. It is only when you see the conditioning and the danger of it immediately, and as you would see a precipice, that you act. So seeing is acting.

Most of us walk through life inattentively, reacting unthinkingly according to the environment in which we have been brought up, and such reactions create only further bondage, further conditioning, but the moment you give your total attention to your conditioning you will see that you are free from the past completely, that it falls away from you naturally.

如果你只把自身局限的危险当作脑中的概念来理解，你是绝不会对它采取行动的。只把危险当作概念来理解，便在概念与行动间制造了冲突，而冲突将耗费你的能量。唯有当你如临深渊般直截了当地看到局限及其危险，你才会立即行动。所以说看到即是行动。

我们大多数人都漫不经心地走完一生，依据自身的成长环境不假思索地反应，而这些反应只会造成更进一步的束缚和限制。然而，一旦你全神贯注于自身的局限，你便会发现自己从过去中彻底解脱了出来，它已轻松自然地离你而去。

PART 3
第三部分

Consciousness—The Totality of
Life—Awareness

意识——生命的整体——觉知

When you become aware of your conditioning you will understand the whole of your consciousness. Consciousness is the total field in which thought functions and relationships exist. All motives, intentions, desires, pleasures, fear, inspiration, longings, hopes, sorrows, joys are in that field. But we have come to divide the consciousness into the active and the dormant, the upper and lower level—that is, all the daily thoughts, feelings and activities on the surface and below them the so-called subconscious, the things with which we are not familiar, which express themselves occasionally through certain intimations, intuitions and dreams.

We are occupied with one little corner of consciousness which is most of our life; the rest, which we call the subconscious, with all its motives, its fears, its racial and inherited qualities, we do not even know how to get into. Now I am asking you, is there such a thing as the subconscious at all? We use that word very freely. We have accepted that there is such a thing and all the phrases and jargon of the analysts and psychologists have seeped into the language; but is there such a thing? And why is it that we give such extraordinary importance to it? It seems to me that it is as trivial and stupid as the conscious mind—as narrow, bigoted, conditioned, anxious and tawdry.

So is it possible to be totally aware of the whole field of consciousness and not merely a part, a fragment, of it? If you are able to be aware of the totality, then you are functioning all the time with your total attention, not partial attention. This is important to understand because when you are

当你开始意识到自身的局限，你方能了解自己意识的整体。意识即是思想得以运转、关系得以存在的那一整片领域。所有的动机、意图、欲望、快乐、恐惧、鼓舞、渴求、希望、悲伤与喜悦，都在那片领域当中。但我们把意识划分成了活跃的和休眠的、上层的和下层的——也就是说，日常所有的思想、感情和行为都在表层，其下则是我们不熟悉的所谓"潜意识"，它们只是偶尔通过某些暗示、直觉和梦境来显露自己。

我们被意识的一个小角落所占据，这便是我们多数人的生活；其余的部分我们称为潜意识，那里涌动着各种动机、恐惧以及种族和遗传的品质，我们甚至都不知道如何进入。而现在我来问你：究竟有没有潜意识这回事？我们非常随意地使用这个词，我们接受了这样东西的存在。心理分析师和心理学家的各类术语和词汇，也已经渗透到了日常的语言中，可是，这样东西究竟存在吗？我们又为何把它看得如此重要？在我看来，它就跟有意识的心智一样微不足道和愚不可及——一样狭隘、偏执、局限、焦虑以及庸俗。

因此，有没有可能全然觉知意识的整个领域，而非只是其中的一个部分、一个碎片？如果可以觉知整体，你就能时时刻刻以全然而非局部的注意力来生活。理解这一点至关重要，因为当你全然觉知意识

being totally aware of the whole field of consciousness there is no friction. It is only when you divide consciousness, which is all thought, feeling and action, into different levels that there is friction.

We live in fragments. You are one thing at the office, another at home; you talk about democracy and in your heart you are autocratic; you talk about loving your neighbours, yet kill him with competition; there is one part of you working, looking, independently of the other. Are you aware of this fragmentary existence in yourself? And is it possible for a brain that has broken up its own functioning, its own thinking, into fragments - is it possible for such a brain to be aware of the whole field? Is it possible to look at the whole of consciousness completely, totally, which means to be a total human being?

If, in order to try to understand the whole structure of the "me", the self, with all its extraordinary complexity, you go step by step, uncovering layer by layer, examining every thought, feeling and motive, you will get caught up in the analytical process which may take you weeks, months, years—and when you admit time into the process of understanding yourself, you must allow for every form of distortion because the self is a complex entity, moving, living, struggling, wanting, denying, with pressures and stresses and influences of all sorts continually at work on it. So you will discover for yourself that this is not the way; you will understand that the only way to look at yourself is totally, immediately, without time; and you can see the totality of yourself only when the mind is not fragmented. What you see in totality is the truth.

Now can you do that? Most of us cannot because most of us have never approached the problem so seriously, because we have never really looked at ourselves. Never. We blame others, we explain things away or we are frightened

的整个领域，摩擦便不复存在。只有当你将意识——所有的思想、感情与行动——划分出各个不同的层面，摩擦才会产生。

我们活得支离破碎：你在办公室是一副样子，回到家便换了副嘴脸；你满口民主，内心却独裁专制；你高谈友爱邻人，却在竞争中将其扼杀；你各方面的工作和面貌，总是相互格格不入。你发觉自己身上的这种支离破碎了吗？而一颗把自身的思想和行为弄得分崩离析的头脑，有没有可能觉知那整片领域？有没有可能全然地、彻底地将意识的整体一览无余，也就是做一个完整的人？

为了解"我"、自我的整个结构，及其复杂无比的各种特性，倘若你打算一步步来，一层层将它揭开，检查每一个想法、感受和动机，你便会陷入分析过程，这或许会花掉你数周、数月、数年的时间。当你容许时间进入自我了解的过程，你就必然为各种扭曲留出了余地，因为自我是个复杂而又鲜活的存在，一直在活动、奋争、渴望、拒绝，各种压力、紧张和影响在不断对它施加作用。因此你自己就会发现这并非解决之道，你会明白观察自己的唯一途径便是整体而直接地去看，决不允许时间进入。而只有你的心不再支离破碎时，你方能将整个自我一览无余。你从整体中所窥见的，便是真理。

那么你能做到吗？我们大多数人都做不到，因为我们从未如此认真地对待这个问题，因为我们从未真正观察过自己。从来没有！我们责怪他人，用解释把事情打发掉，或者害怕去看自己。但是，当你完整地去看，你就会付出你全部的注意力、你的整个生命、你的一切——你的眼睛、你的耳朵、你的每一条神经；你会完全摒弃自我，

to look. But when you look totally you will give your whole attention, your whole being, everything of yourself, your eyes, your ears, your nerves; you will attend with complete self-abandonment, and then there is no room for fear, no room for contradiction, and therefore no conflict.

Attention is not the same thing as concentration. Concentration is exclusion; attention, which is total awareness, excludes nothing. It seems to me that most of us are not aware, not only of what we are talking about but of our environment, the colours around us, the people, the shape of the trees, the clouds, the movement of water. Perhaps it is because we are so concerned with ourselves, with our own petty little problems, our own ideas, our own pleasures, pursuits and ambitions that we are not objectively aware. And yet we talk a great deal about awareness.

Once in India I was travelling in a car. There was a chauffeur driving and I was sitting beside him. There were three gentlemen behind discussing awareness very intently and asking me questions about awareness, and unfortunately at that moment the driver was looking somewhere else and he ran over a goat, and the three gentlemen were still discussing awareness —totally unaware that they had run over a goat. When the lack of attention was pointed out to those gentlemen who were trying to be aware it was a great surprise to them.

And with most of us it is the same. We are not aware of outward things or of inward things. If you want to understand the beauty of a bird, a fly, or a leaf, or a person with all his complexities, you have to give your whole attention which is awareness. And you can give your whole attention only when you care, which means that you really love to understand - then you give your whole heart and mind to find out.

Such awareness is like living with a snake in the room; you watch its

全神贯注，此时便完全没有了恐惧和矛盾的余地，冲突也将因此不复存在。

关注与专注并不是同一回事。专注是排斥性的，而关注则是全然的觉知，它不排斥任何东西。在我看来，我们大多数人都没有觉察力，不仅对我们所谈的事情，而且对周围的环境、色彩、人群、树木的轮廓、云朵以及流水都无知无觉。原因或许是我们都太关心自己了，关心自己各种微不足道的问题，自己的观点、自己的快乐、追求以及野心，导致我们无法客观地觉知。可同时我们又在大谈觉知。

有一次在印度，我们乘车旅行，司机在驾驶，我就坐他旁边。后座有三位先生正在热烈地探讨觉知，不时问我有关觉知的各种问题。这时不幸的事发生了，司机因为走神撞上了一头山羊，可那三位先生还在讨论觉知，完全没注意到他们碾过了一头山羊。他们努力保持觉知，却又是那么缺乏警觉，当我指出这一点时，他们感到惊讶万分。

而我们大部分人的情形都如出一辙，我们对外在或内在发生的事都浑然不觉。若想了解一只鸟、一个飞虫、一片树叶或者一个极为复杂的人的美丽之处，你就得付出全部的注意力，也就是觉知。只有当你怀抱关爱之心，当你真的乐于去了解时，你方能全神贯注，此时你就会付出自己的全部身心与头脑去探明真相。

这样的觉知就如同与毒蛇共处一室，你注视它的一举一动，你对它发出的最轻微的声响都非常、非常敏感。这样的全神贯注便是完整的能量，在这份觉知当中，你的整个自我瞬间即可显露无遗。

若你如此深入地观察过自己，你便可以探索得更为深远。我们

every movement, you are very, very sensitive to the slightest sound it makes. Such a state of attention is total energy; in such awareness the totality of yourself is revealed in an instant.

When you have looked at yourself so deeply you can go much deeper. When we use the word "deeper" we are not being comparative. We think in comparisons—deep and shallow, happy and unhappy. We are always measuring, comparing. Now is there such a state as the shallow and the deep in oneself? When I say, "My mind is shallow, petty, narrow, limited", how do I know all these things? Because I have compared my mind with your mind which is brighter, has more capacity, is more intelligent and alert. Do I know my pettiness without comparison? When I am hungry, I do not compare that hunger with yesterday's hunger. Yesterday's hunger is an idea, a memory.

If I am all the time measuring myself against you, struggling to be like you, then I am denying what I am myself. Therefore I am creating an illusion. When I have understood that comparison in any form leads only to greater illusion and greater misery, just as when I analyse myself, add to my knowledge of myself bit by bit, or identify myself with something outside myself, whether it be the State, a saviour or an ideology—when I understand that all such processes lead only to greater conformity and therefore greater conflict—when I see all this I put it completely away. Then my mind is no longer seeking. It is very important to understand this. Then my mind is no longer groping, searching, questioning. This does not mean that my mind is satisfied with things as they are, but such a mind has no illusion. Such a mind can then move in a totally different dimension. The dimension in which we usually live, the life of every day which is pain, pleasure and fear, has conditioned the mind, limited the nature of the mind, and when that pain, pleasure and fear have gone (which does not mean that

所用的"更深"一词，并不带有比较的意味。我们通常以比较的方式思考——深与浅，快乐与不快乐，我们总是在衡量、比较。然而，我们内心真的有一种所谓肤浅或者深刻的状态吗？当我说："我的心智肤浅、渺小、狭隘、局限"，我是怎么知道这些的？因为我拿自己的心智跟你的心智比较了一番，你更聪明、更能干、更智慧、更敏锐。如果不比较，我还知道自己渺小吗？如果我饿了，我是不会把那种饥饿与昨天的饥饿做比较的，昨天的饥饿已经变成一个概念、一个记忆了。

如果我老是拿你来衡量自己，努力变得跟你一样，我就是在否定真实的自己，因而编织了一个幻觉。任何形式的比较都只会导致更大的幻觉、更多的痛苦。那就如同分析自己，一点点添加关于自己的知识一样，或者让自己认同某种更伟大的外在事物，无论是国家、救世主还是理念。当我懂得了所有此类过程只会导致更严重的服从，进而会招来更严重的冲突，当我看清了这一切，我就会将比较彻底摒弃，我的心于是不再追寻。理解这一点真的至关重要。于是我的心不再探求、追寻、发问。并不是说我的心满足于现状，而是说这样的心不再抱有任何幻想，进而便能向另一个截然不同的维度进发了。我们通常所生活的维度，这种充斥着痛苦、快感和恐惧的日常生活，制约了心灵，局限了心的本性。当那些痛苦、快感和恐惧都已消失不见（并不是说你不再拥有喜悦，喜悦跟快感有天壤之别），心便会在另一个维度运转，那里毫无冲突，也没有所谓的"分别感"。

用语言来表达，我们只能说到这里了，那超越的存在无法诉诸文

you no longer have joy: joy is something entirely different from pleasure) —then the mind functions in a different dimension in which there is no conflict, no sense of "otherness".

Verbally we can go only so far: what lies beyond cannot be put into words because the word is not the thing. Up to now we can describe, explain, but no words or explanations can open the door. What will open the door is daily awareness and attention—awareness of how we speak, what we say, how we walk, what we think. It is like cleaning a room and keeping it in order. Keeping the room in order is important in one sense but totally unimportant in another. There must be order in the room but order will not open the door or the window. What will open the door is not your volition or desire. You cannot possibly invite the other.

All that you can do is to keep the room in order, which is to be virtuous for itself, not for what it will bring. To be sane, rational, orderly. Then perhaps, if you are lucky, the window will open and the breeze will come in. Or it may not. It depends on the state of your mind. And that state of mind can be understood only by yourself, by watching it and never trying to shape it, never taking sides, never opposing, never agreeing, never justifying, never condemning, never judging—which means watching it without any choice. And out of this choiceless awareness perhaps the door will open and you will know what that dimension is in which there is no conflict and no time.

字，因为文字并非事物本身。到目前为止，我们还可以描述与解释，但任何文字或解释都无法开启那扇门。能开启那扇门的，是日常的觉知与关注——觉知我们如何讲话、如何走路，觉知我们的所言、所想。那就像是打扫一个房间，让它井井有条。一方面可以说，让房间井井有条非常重要，另一方面也可以说完全不重要。房间必须整洁有序，但秩序并不会开启那扇门、那扇窗。开启那扇门的，也并非你的决心或者愿望。你是无法主动邀约那"另一个事物"的。

你所能做的，就只有让房间整洁有序，保持自身的美德，却不是为了得到什么。保持健全、清明、有序，然后，如果你够幸运，或许窗户便会打开，微风便会进来。又或许不会。这取决于你的心智状态。而你的心智状态唯有你自己能了解——通过观察它，却从不试图塑造它，从不采取立场，既不反对也不赞同，既不辩解也不谴责，丝毫不做评判——也就是毫无选择地观察它。从这份无选择的觉察中，也许大门瞬间即会敞开，你便可一览那毫无冲突而又超越时间的维度。

PART 4
第四部分

We said in the last chapter that joy was something entirely different from pleasure, so let us find out what is involved in pleasure and whether it is at all possible to live in a world that does not contain pleasure but a tremendous sense of joy, of bliss.

We are all engaged in the pursuit of pleasure in some form or other —intellectual, sensuous or cultural pleasure, the pleasure of reforming, telling others what to do, of modifying the evils of society, of doing good —the pleasure of greater knowledge, greater physical satisfaction, greater experience, greater understanding of life, all the clever, cunning things of the mind - and the ultimate pleasure is, of course, to have God.

Pleasure is the structure of society. From childhood until death we are secretly, cunningly or obviously pursuing pleasure. So whatever our form of pleasure is, I think we should be very clear about it because it is going to guide and shape our lives. It is therefore important for each one of us to investigate closely, hesitantly and delicately this question of pleasure, for to find pleasure, and then nourish and sustain it, is a basic demand of life and without it existence becomes dull, stupid, lonely and meaningless.

You may ask why then should life not be guided by pleasure? For the very simple reason that pleasure must bring pain, frustration, sorrow and fear, and, out of fear, violence. If you want to live that way, live that way. Most of the world does, anyway, but if you want to be free from sorrow you must understand the whole structure of pleasure.

上一章我们说过，喜悦同快感有天壤之别，所以我们这就来搞清楚快感的含义，以及究竟是否可能活在一个不包含快感，却极度喜悦与幸福的世界。

我们都致力于追逐各种形式的快感——思想上的、肉体上的或是文化上的快感，革新、吩咐别人做事、改良社会弊病、行善的快感，以及拥有更多知识、获得更多身体满足、更多经验、对人生更深刻领悟的快感，心智各种聪明、狡猾的伎俩带来的快感，当然，还有终极的快感——拥有上帝。

快感乃是社会的基本构架，从生到死，我们都在隐蔽地、狡猾地或者明目张胆地追逐快感。因此，无论我们追求的快感是何种形式，我想我们都应该彻底看清它，因为它将指引和塑造我们的人生。所以，密切地、谨慎地、细致地审视快感这个问题，对我们每个人来说都非常重要。因为寻找然后滋养和维系快感，是一个基本的生活需要，如果没有它，生活似乎就会变得枯燥、愚蠢、孤寂，乃至毫无意义。

你或许会问，生活为何就不应由快感来主导呢？原因非常简单：快感必定会招来痛苦、沮丧、悲伤与恐惧，而恐惧会导致暴力。倘若你甘愿过那样的生活，那就去过好了。不管怎样，大部分世人确实如

To understand pleasure is not to deny it. We are not condemning it or saying it is right or wrong, but if we pursue it, let us do so with our eyes open, knowing that a mind that is all the time seeking pleasure must inevitably find its shadow, pain. They cannot be separated, although we run after pleasure and try to avoid pain.

Now, why is the mind always demanding pleasure? Why is it that we do noble and ignoble things with the undercurrent of pleasure? Why is it we sacrifice and suffer on the thin thread of pleasure? What is pleasure and how does it come into being? I wonder if any of you have asked yourself these questions and followed the answers to the very end?

Pleasure comes into being through four stages—perception, sensation, contact and desire. I see a beautiful motor car, say; then I get a sensation, a reaction, from looking at it; then I touch it or imagine touching it, and then there is the desire to own and show myself off in it. Or I see a lovely cloud, or a mountain clear against the sky, or a leaf that has just come in springtime, or a deep valley full of loveliness and splendour, or a glorious sunset, or a beautiful face, intelligent, alive, not self-conscious and therefore no longer beautiful.

I look at these things with intense delight and as I observe them there is no observer but only sheer beauty like love. For a moment I am absent with all my problems, anxieties and miseries—there is only that marvellous thing. I can look at it with joy and the next moment forget it, or else the mind steps in, and then the problem begins; my mind thinks over what it has seen and thinks how beautiful it was; I tell myself I should like to see it again many times. Thought begins to compare, judge, and say "I must have it again tomorrow". The continuity of an experience that has given delight for a second is sustained by thought.

此。然而，如果你想摆脱痛苦，你就必须了解快感的全部来龙去脉。

了解快感，并不是要否认它。我们既不是在谴责它，也不是说它是对是错，而是如果要探究它，我们就必须圆睁双眼，看清这一点：一颗不停寻求快感的心，必定会招来痛苦与阴影。苦乐密不可分，尽管我们总想趋乐避苦。

那么，心为何始终要寻求快感呢？为什么我们会受快感的暗流推动，做出各种高尚与卑鄙的事来？为何我们的牺牲与苦难，都要悬于快感这一线之上？快感是什么，它又是如何产生的？我想知道你们当中可曾有人问过自己这些问题，并将答案追究到底？

快感的产生有四个阶段——知觉，感受，接触以及欲望。比如说，我看到一台漂亮的汽车；看到之后，就产生了一种感受、一种反应；然后我触摸它，或者想象自己触摸它；然后便有了想要拥有它、坐进去炫耀自己的欲望。又比如说，我看到一朵美丽的云，蓝天下一座清朗的山峰，春天新绽的一片嫩叶，秀美辉煌的一条深谷，一场壮丽的日落，或是一张俊俏的脸庞，机灵、生动，毫不忸怩从而不失美丽。

我看着这些，心情极为愉悦，此时没有观察者，只有纯粹的美与爱。有那么一刻，我，连同我所有的问题、焦虑和痛苦，统统不见了，只剩那件美丽非凡的事物。我可以心怀喜悦地看着它，下一刻就把它抛诸脑后；抑或，头脑插手进来，于是麻烦便开始了。脑子反刍它所见到的，回想那有多么美，然后告诉自己：我还想反反复复地见到它。思想开始了比较、判断，然后说："我明天一定要再次看

It is the same with sexual desire or any other form of desire. There is nothing wrong with desire. To react is perfectly normal. If you stick a pin in me I shall react unless I am paralysed. But then thought steps in and chews over the delight and turns it into pleasure. Thought wants to repeat the experience, and the more you repeat, the more mechanical it becomes; the more you think about it, the more strength thought gives to pleasure. So thought creates and sustains pleasure through desire, and gives it continuity, and therefore the natural reaction of desire to any beautiful thing is perverted by thought. Thought turns it into a memory and memory is then nourished by thinking about it over and over again.

Of course, memory has a place at a certain level. In everyday life we could not function at all without it. In its own field it must be efficient but there is a state of mind where it has very little place. A mind which is not crippled by memory has real freedom.

Have you ever noticed that when you respond to something totally, with all your heart, there is very little memory? It is only when you do not respond to a challenge with your whole being that there is a conflict, a struggle, and this brings confusion and pleasure or pain. And the struggle breeds memory. That memory is added to all the time by other memories and it is those memories which respond. Anything that is the result of memory is old and therefore never free. There is no such thing as freedom of thought. It is sheer nonsense.

Thought is never new, for thought is the response of memory, experience, knowledge. Thought, because it is old, makes this thing which you have looked at with delight and felt tremendously for the moment, old. From the old you derive pleasure, never from the new. There is no time in the new.

到。"曾经带来刹那愉悦的一次经验，就这样被思想维系着，从而延续了下去。

性欲或是其他形式的欲望也是如此。欲望本身并没有错，起反应也是极其正常的事。如果你拿针扎我，我立刻便会反应，除非我瘫痪了。但是，随后思想涉足进来，咀嚼那份喜悦，然后把它变成了快感。思想希望重复经验，而你越是重复，就会变得越机械；你越是回想，念头就会让快感越强烈。所以，是思想借助欲望制造并维系了快感，让它得以延续。因此，对于美好事物产生的原本自然的需求反应，就这样被思想败坏了。思想把它变成了记忆，记忆又因为一遍遍的回想而得到了滋养。

当然，记忆在一定层面上是有其作用的。在日常生活中，如果没有记忆，我们根本无法运转。它在自己的领域内，必须充分发挥作用，但是在另一种心智状态下，它就没什么地位了。而一颗未被记忆所残害的心，才拥有真正的自由。

你可曾注意到，当你对某件事完整地、全心全意地做出回应时，留下的记忆就会非常少？只有当你没有全身心地应对挑战时，才会产生冲突与挣扎，而这就带来了困惑、快乐或者痛苦。正是这份挣扎滋生了记忆，它又被另外的记忆不断累加，做出回应的正是这些记忆。凡是记忆的产物，就必定是陈旧的，因而绝无可能是自由的。根本没有"思想自由"这回事，那纯属无稽之谈。

思想从来不是新鲜的，因为它是记忆、经验、知识的反应。因为思想是陈旧的，所以它把你在那一刻满怀喜悦看到与强烈感受到的东

So if you can look at all things without allowing pleasure to creep in—at a face, a bird, the colour of a sari, the beauty of a sheet of water shimmering in the sun, or anything that gives delight—if you can look at it without wanting the experience to be repeated, then there will be no pain, no fear, and therefore tremendous joy.

It is the struggle to repeat and perpetuate pleasure which turns it into pain. Watch it in yourself. The very demand for the repetition of pleasure brings about pain, because it is not the same, as it was yesterday. You struggle to achieve the same delight, not only to your aesthetic sense but the same inward quality of the mind, and you are hurt and disappointed because it is denied to you.

Have you observed what happens to you when you are denied a little pleasure? When you don't get what you want you become anxious, envious, hateful. Have you noticed when you have been denied the pleasure of drinking or smoking or sex or whatever it is—have you noticed what battles you go through? And all that is a form of fear, isn't it? You are afraid of not getting what you want or of losing what you have. When some particular faith or ideology which you have held for years is shaken or torn away from you by logic or life, aren'st you afraid of standing alone? That belief has for years given you satisfaction and pleasure, and when it is taken away you are left stranded, empty, and the fear remains until you find another form of pleasure, another belief.

It seems to me so simple and because it is so simple we refuse to see its simplicity. We like to complicate everything. When your wife turns away from you, aren't you jealous? Aren't you angry? Don't you hate the man who has attracted her? And what is all that but fear of losing something which has given you a great deal of pleasure, a companionship, a certain

西，也变得陈旧了。你只能从陈旧而非崭新的事物中汲取快感，新事物中根本没有时间的存在。

因此，如果你能放眼万物——一张脸庞，一只小鸟，一件纱丽的色彩，阳光下闪闪发亮的一袭水面，或是任何带来愉悦的事物——却不让快感悄悄潜入，如果你能看着它，却不希望重温那种体验，那么痛苦与恐惧将无从生起，因而就有了无尽的喜悦。

正是重温以及无止境延续快感的努力，将快乐变成了痛苦。请在自己身上观察这一点。重复快感的需求本身便带来了痛苦，因为今天的感受不可能与昨日相同。你努力获取同等的愉悦，不仅是那份美感，而且还要心灵具备同样的内在品质，结果却因为愿望无法达成而伤心失望。

你可曾观察过，哪怕是一点点小小的快乐遭到了拒绝，你会怎么样？当你得不到你想要的，你就会变得焦躁、嫉妒、怨恨。你可曾注意到，当你想得到抽烟、喝酒、性欲或是无论什么快感，却遭到拒绝时，你内心会经历怎样的挣扎？这都是恐惧的表现，不是吗？你害怕得不到自己想要的，也害怕失去自己所拥有的。当你抱守多年的特定信仰或理念，被逻辑或是被生活所动摇、所剥离，你难道不害怕孤立于世吗？那个信仰多年来一直让你快乐又满足，当它被夺去，你落得进退维谷、空虚无依，于是恐惧进驻内心，直到你找到另一种快感、另一种信仰为止。

这点在我看来实在是太简单了，也正因为如此，我们拒绝去看这份简单，我们喜欢把一切都弄得很复杂。如果你妻子弃你而去，你难

quality of assurance and the satisfaction of possession?

So if you understand that where there is a search for pleasure there must be pain, live that way if you want to, but don't just slip into it. If you want to end pleasure, though, which is to end pain, you must be totally attentive to the whole structure of pleasure—not cut it out as monks and sannyasis do, never looking at a woman because they think it is a sin and thereby destroying the vitality of their understanding—but seeing the whole meaning and significance of pleasure. Then you will have tremendous joy in life. You cannot think about joy. Joy is an immediate thing and by thinking about it, you turn it into pleasure. Living in the present is the instant perception of beauty and the great delight in it without seeking pleasure from it.

道不嫉妒、不生气吗？你难道不痛恨那个诱惑她的男人吗？你不过是害怕失去她曾经带给你的巨大快感、陪伴、安全感，以及占有的满足感，除此之外，哪里还有别的？

因此，如果你明白只要追逐快感，痛苦便在所难免，那么只要你乐意，就那样活着好了，只是当心不要就那样陷进去。而如果你想终止快感——实际上便是终止痛苦——你就必须全神贯注地观察快感的整个构造。并非像修道士和托钵僧那样戒除快感——决不能看女人，因为他们认为那是罪过，那样会毁掉他们领悟的生命力——而是看清快感的全部内涵和意义，然后你才能体会生命中无边的喜悦。你不能思考喜悦，喜悦属于当下，如果思考它，你就把它变成了快感。"活在当下"便是瞬间洞察当下的美与狂喜，却不从中寻求快感。

PART 5
第五部分

Before we go any further I would like to ask you what is your fundamental, lasting interest in life? Putting all oblique answers aside and dealing with this question directly and honestly, what would you answer? Do you know?

Isn't it yourself? Anyway, that is what most of us would say if we answered truthfully. I am interested in my progress, my job, my family, the little corner in which I live, in getting a better position for myself, more prestige, more power, more domination over others and so on. I think it would be logical, wouldn't it, to admit to ourselves that that is what most of us are primarily interested in—"me" first?

Some of us would say that it is wrong to be primarily interested in ourselves. But what is wrong about it except that we seldom decently, honestly, admit it? If we do, we are rather ashamed of it. So there it is—one is fundamentally interested in oneself, and for various ideological or traditional reasons one thinks it is wrong. But what one thinks is irrelevant. Why introduce the factor of its being wrong? That is an idea, a concept. What is a fact is that one is fundamentally and lastingly interested in oneself.

You may say that it is more satisfactory to help another than to think about yourself. What is the difference? It is still self-concern. If it gives you greater satisfaction to help others, you are concerned about what will give you greater satisfaction. Why bring any ideological concept into it? Why this double thinking? Why not say, "What I really want is satisfaction, whether

在我们继续往下进行之前，我想问一问：生活中你最主要、最持久的关注点是什么？抛开各种拐弯抹角的回答，直截了当地面对这个问题，你会如何作答？你知道吗？

难道不是你自己吗？不管怎样，这就是大部分人的回答，倘若我们诚实的话。我关心我的进步、我的工作、我的家庭、我所生活的那个小角落，我想得到更高的地位、威望、权势，以及对他人更大的支配权，等等。我想，"我"字当先——这便是我们大多数人最主要的兴趣所在，坦承这一点，是顺理成章的，不是吗？

有些人会说，主要关心自己是不对的。可是，除了我们很少正直地坦承这点以外，那又有什么不对呢？如果承认，我们会觉得相当羞耻。总之，事实便是如此——人最感兴趣的就是自己。而由于各种观念上的、传统的原因，人们认为那是错的。但是一个人怎么认为并不重要，那为什么还要引入"那是错的"这个看法？那不过是一个观点、一个概念罢了。事实就是：人基本上一直就是对自己最感兴趣。

你或许会说，帮助别人比为自己着想，更令人满足。可那又有什么区别呢？你关心的依旧是自己。如果帮助别人带给你更多满足，你关心的还是什么会令你更满足。为何要引入意识形态上的观念？为何有这种双重思维？为何不直接说："我真正想要的就是满足，无论是

in sex, or in helping others, or in becoming a great saint, scientist or politician"? It is the same process, isn't it? Satisfaction in all sorts of ways, subtle and obvious, is what we want. When we say we want freedom we want it because we think it may be wonderfully satisfying, and the ultimate satisfaction, of course, is this peculiar idea of self-realization. What we are really seeking is a satisfaction in which there is no dissatisfaction at all.

Most of us crave the satisfaction of having a position in society because we are afraid of being nobody. Society is so constructed that a citizen who has a position of respect is treated with great courtesy, whereas a man who has no position is kicked around. Everyone in the world wants a position, whether in society, in the family or to sit on the right hand of God, and this position must be recognized by others, otherwise it is no position at all. We must always sit on the platform. Inwardly we are whirlpools of misery and mischief and therefore to be regarded outwardly as a great figure is very gratifying. This craving for position, for prestige, for power, to be recognized by society as being outstanding in some way, is a wish to dominate others, and this wish to dominate is a form of aggression. The saint who seeks a position in regard to his saintliness is as aggressive as the chicken pecking in the farmyard. And what is the cause of this aggressiveness? It is fear, isn't it?

Fear is one of the greatest problems in life. A mind that is caught in fear lives in confusion, in conflict, and therefore must be violent, distorted and aggressive. It dare not move away from its own patterns of thinking, and this breeds hypocrisy. Until we are free from fear, climb the highest mountain, invent every kind of God, we will always remain in darkness.

Living in such a corrupt, stupid society as we do, with the competitive education we receive which engenders fear, we are all burdened with fears of

性，是帮助别人，还是成为伟大的圣人、科学家或者政治家"？那都是同一个过程，不是吗？各种形式的满足，无论隐蔽还是明显，就是我们想要的。我们都说希望得到自由，那是因为我们以为自由或许能令人极度满足。当然了，最终极的满足便是"自我实现"这个古怪的想法了。我们实际上追求的就是没有任何不满的一种满足感。

我们大多数人都渴望在社会上拥有一席之地，因为我们害怕自己一无所是。社会的结构便是如此：位高权重的人即可享有无上礼遇，而没有地位的人则被呼来喝去。世上的每个人都希望获得某种地位，无论是社会地位、家庭地位，还是坐在上帝右手的地位，并且这个地位必须为他人所公认，否则就根本算不上地位了。我们必须始终端坐高台之上。由于内心满是悲伤与不幸的旋涡，因此被外界当作大人物会令我们非常满足。这种对地位、威望、权力的追求，在某方面被社会视为杰出人物的渴望，是为了主宰他人，而这种主宰的愿望正是侵略性的表现。寻求神圣地位的圣人所具有的侵略性，与农家庭院里争抢啄食的小鸡并无二致。而又是什么导致了这种侵略性？不正是恐惧吗？

恐惧是生命中最为庞大的问题之一。深陷恐惧之中的心，活在困惑与冲突当中，因此必定是暴力、扭曲以及颇具攻击性的。它不敢偏离自己的思维模式，而这导致了虚伪。除非我们摆脱了恐惧，否则即使爬上最高的山峰、发明出各路神明，我们仍将长久地滞留在黑暗当中。

我们活在如此腐朽、如此愚蠢的社会上，接受了充满竞争进而催

some kind, and fear is a dreadful thing which warps, twists and dulls our days.

There is physical fear but that is a response we have inherited from the animals. It is psychological fears we are concerned with here, for when we understand the deep-rooted psychological fears we will be able to meet the animal fears, whereas to be concerned with the animal fears first will never help us to understand the psychological fears.

We are all afraid about something; there is no fear in abstraction, it is always in relation to something. Do you know your own fears—fear of losing your job, of not having enough food or money, or what your neighbours or the public think about you, or not being a success, of losing your position in society, of being despised or ridiculed—fear of pain and disease, of domination, of never knowing what love is or of not being loved, of losing your wife or children, of death, of living in a world that is like death, of utter boredom, of not living up to the image others have built about you, of losing your faith—all these and innumerable other fears—do you know your own particular fears? And what do you usually do about them? You run away from them, don't you, or invent ideas and images to cover them? But to run away from fear is only to increase it.

One of the major causes of fear is that we do not want to face ourselves as we are. So, as well as the fears themselves, we have to examine the network of escapes we have developed to rid ourselves of them. If the mind, in which is included the brain, tries to overcome fear, to suppress it, discipline it, control it, translate it into terms of something else, there is friction, there is conflict, and that conflict is a waste of energy.

The first thing to ask ourselves then is what is fear and how does it arise? What do we mean by the word fear itself? I am asking myself what is fear not what I am afraid of.

生恐惧的教育，我们都背负着恐惧的重担。而恐惧这可怕的东西已将我们的日子变得扭曲、败坏而又阴郁。

我们确有身体上的恐惧，但那是从动物身上遗传下来的本能反应，而在这里，我们关注的是心理上的恐惧。因为，当我们看清了根深蒂固的心理恐惧，才有能力应对动物性的恐惧。反之，若是先处理动物性的恐惧，则绝无可能帮我们看清心理上的恐惧。

我们都对某种东西怀有恐惧，抽象的恐惧并不存在，恐惧总是与某个对象有关。你是否熟悉自己的恐惧——害怕丢掉工作，害怕食不果腹，害怕金钱匮乏，害怕邻居或公众对你的看法，害怕不能成功，害怕丧失社会地位，害怕遭人鄙视、受人讥笑，害怕痛苦与疾病，害怕被人主宰，害怕不知何为爱或是没人爱你，害怕失去妻子或孩子，害怕死亡，害怕活在一个死气沉沉、极端乏味的世界上，害怕辜负别人为你塑造的光辉形象，害怕失去信仰，诸如此类以及不计其数的其他恐惧——你熟悉自己那些特定的恐惧吗？你通常又会如何处置它们？你逃避它们，或是发明出各种理念和意象来掩盖它们，不是吗？然而逃避恐惧只会令恐惧增强。

恐惧的一大肇因，即是我们不愿面对真实的自己。因此，除了各种恐惧本身，我们也必须审视为了消除恐惧我们所编织的逃避网络。只要心灵——包括头脑——试图克服恐惧，或是压抑它、约束它、控制它、转化它，就会造成摩擦和冲突，而冲突正是能量的浪费。

那么，我们首先要问自己的问题便是：什么是恐惧，以及它是如何产生的？我们所说的"恐惧"一词，本身是何含义？我现在问自己

I lead a certain kind of life; I think in a certain pattern; I have certain beliefs and dogmas and I don't want those patterns of existence to be disturbed because I have my roots in them. I don't want them to be disturbed because the disturbance produces a state of unknowing and I dislike that. If I am torn away from everything I know and believe, I want to be reasonably certain of the state of things to which I am going. So the brain cells have created a pattern and those brain cells refuse to create another pattern which may be uncertain. The movement from certainty to uncertainty is what I call fear.

At the actual moment as I am sitting here I am not afraid; I am not afraid in the present, nothing is happening to me, nobody is threatening me or taking anything away from me. But beyond the actual moment there is a deeper layer in the mind which is consciously or unconsciously thinking of what might happen in the future or worrying that something from the past may overtake me. So I am afraid of the past and of the future. I have divided time into the past and the future. Thought steps in, says, "Be careful it does not happen again", or "Be prepared for the future. The future may be dangerous for you. You have got something now but you may lose it. You may die tomorrow, your wife may run away, you may lose your job. You may never become famous. You may be lonely. You want to be quite sure of tomorrow."

Now take your own particular form of fear. Look at it. Watch your reactions to it. Can you look at it without any movement of escape, justification, condemnation or suppression? Can you look at that fear without the word which causes the fear? Can you look at death, for instance, without the word which arouses the fear of death? The word itself brings a tremor, doesn't it, as the word love has its own tremor, its own image? Now is the image you have in your mind about death, the

的，是何为恐惧，而非我恐惧的对象是什么。

我过着某种生活，我以某种模式思考，我抱持某些信仰与教条，我不希望这些生活模式受到打扰，因为我扎根于其中。我不希望它们受到打扰，因为打扰会带来一种未知状态，我不喜欢那样。如果我熟悉与相信的一切都要被剥离，我便需要对自己将要去到的境界，有相当确定的把握。所以说脑细胞塑造了一个模式，同时拒绝建立另一个或许不太确定的模式。从确定到不确定的那种活动，我就称之为"恐惧"。

此刻坐在这里，我没有恐惧；此刻我并不害怕，没什么事发生，也没什么人威胁我或是抢劫我。但是，离开了当下，内心深处便在有意无意地思量将来会发生什么，或是担忧过往发生的事会再次降临到我身上。所以我害怕的是过去和未来，我把时间划分成了过去和未来。此时念头插手进来，说："当心，别让它再发生"，或者，"要为将来准备，未来或许危机四伏。你现在拥有的，以后也许会失去。明天你可能会死掉，妻子可能会跑掉，你可能会失业。你可能永远也出不了名，你可能会孤寂一生。因此，你希望对明天有十足的把握"。

现在就拿起你个人特定的恐惧看一看，同时观察自己对它的反应。你能否看着它，而没有丝毫逃避、辩解、谴责或压抑的活动？你能否看着那份恐惧，而不想着会招来恐惧的词语？比如说，你能否正视死亡，却不想着会唤起对死亡的恐惧的词语？"死亡"一词本身便会带来一种战栗，就像"爱"这个词也会带来战栗与意象一样，不是

memory of so many deaths you have seen and the associating of yourself with those incidents—is it that image which is creating fear? Or are you actually afraid of coming to an end, not of the image creating the end? Is the word death causing you fear or the actual ending? If it is the word or the memory which is causing you fear then it is not fear at all.

You were ill two years ago, let us say, and the memory of that pain, that illness, remains, and the memory now functioning says, "Be careful, don't get ill, again". So the memory with its associations is creating fear, and that is not fear at all because actually at the moment you have very good health. Thought, which is always old, because thought is the response of memory and memories are always old—thought creates, in time, the feeling that you are afraid which is not an actual fact. The actual fact is that you are well. But the experience, which has remained in the mind as a memory, rouses the thought, "Be careful, don't fall ill again".

So we see that thought engenders one kind of fear. But is there fear at all apart from that? Is fear always the result of thought and, if it is, is there any other form of fear? We are afraid of death—that is, something that is going to happen tomorrow or the day after tomorrow, in time. There is a distance between actuality and what will be. Now thought has experienced this state; by observing death it says, "I am going to die." Thought creates the fear of death, and if it doesn'is there any fear at all?

Is fear the result of thought? If it is, thought being always old, fear is always old. As we have said, there is no new thought. If we recognise it, it is already old. So what we are afraid of is the repetition of the old—the thought of what has been projecting into the future. Therefore thought is responsible for fear. This is so, you can see it for yourself. When you are confronted with something immediately there is no fear. It is only when

吗？那么，你心中对死亡所怀有的意象，你所目睹的无数死亡，以及把自己与那些事件联系在一起——是否正是这些意象造成了恐惧？还是说，你是真的在恐惧生命的终结，而非构想出终结的那个意象？令你恐惧的，是"死亡"一词，还是实际的生命终结？若是那个词或者那个记忆令你恐惧，那就根本不是真正的恐惧。

假如说你两年前生过病，对病痛、疾病的记忆留存了下来，而此刻那份记忆正起着作用，说："当心，别再生病了！"所以说，是记忆以及联想造成了恐惧，可那根本不是真正的恐惧，因为你此刻实际上非常健康。思想始终是老旧不堪的，因为思想是记忆产生的反应，而记忆永远是陈旧的。思想借助时间，捏造出你很害怕的感觉，可那根本不是事实。事实上你好得很。但是，作为记忆留存在心中的经验，唤起了这个念头："当心，别再生病了。"

因此，我们看清了是思想引发了某种恐惧。但是，除此之外，究竟还有没有其他恐惧存在？恐惧是否永远是思想的产物，如果是，那还有其他类型的恐惧吗？我们恐惧死亡——某件明天、后天或某个时候会发生的事，事实与未来之间便有一个距离。思想经历过这种情境，通过观察死亡，它说："我也会死。"是念头造成了对死亡的恐惧，如果它不制造恐惧，那么恐惧还会存在吗？

恐惧是不是思想的产物？如果是，因为思想始终是陈旧的，那么恐惧也始终是陈旧的。正如我们所说，并不存在新鲜的思想，只要我们认出了它，它就必定是陈旧的。因此，我们所恐惧的是旧事重现——把已然如何的想法投射到了将来。所以说思想要为恐惧负责，

thought comes in that there is fear.

Therefore our question now is, is it possible for the mind to live completely, totally, in the present? It is only such a mind that has no fear. But to understand this, you have to understand the structure of thought, memory and time. And in understanding it, understanding not intellectually, not verbally, but actually with your heart, your mind, your guts, you will be free from fear; then the mind can use thought without creating fear.

Thought, like memory, is, of course, necessary for daily living. It is the only instrument we have for communication, working at our jobs and so forth. Thought is the response to memory, memory which has been accumulated through experience, knowledge, tradition, time. And from this background of memory we react and this reaction is thinking. So thought is essential at certain levels but when thought projects itself psychologically as the future and the past, creating fear as well as pleasure, the mind is made dull and therefore inaction is inevitable.

So I ask myself, "Why, why, why, do I think about the future and the past in terms of pleasure and pain, knowing that such thought creates fear? Isn't it possible for thought psychologically to stop, for otherwise fear will never end?"

One of the functions of thought is to be occupied all the time with something. Most of us want to have our minds continually occupied so that we are prevented from seeing ourselves as we actually are. We are afraid to be empty. We are afraid to look at our fears.

Consciously you can be aware of your fears but at the deeper levels of your mind are you aware of them? And how are you going to find out the fears that are hidden, secret? Is fear to be divided into the conscious and the subconscious? This is a very important question. The specialist,

事实就是如此，你可以亲自看到这一点。当你直截了当地面对某事，恐惧就不存在，只有当思想介入进来，你才会恐惧。

因此，我们现在的问题是：心是否可能完全地、彻底地活在当下？唯有这样的一颗心才无所畏惧。但若要了解这一点，你就必须了解思想、记忆以及时间的架构。这份了解并非道理上的、字面上的，而是用你的全副身心真正发自肺腑地领会它，这样你方能从恐惧中解脱。此时你的心便可以运用思想却不会造成恐惧。

思想就像记忆一样，对于日常生活当然是必不可少的，它是我们用来交流、用来工作等的唯一工具。思想乃是对记忆的反应，而记忆是通过经验、知识、传统和时间积累而来的。我们根据记忆的背景做出反应，这反应便是思想。所以说思想在某些层面上是不可或缺的。然而，一旦思想从心理上将自己化身为过去和未来，制造了快感与恐惧，心智就会变得迟钝，了无生气于是成为必然。

因此，我追问自己："这究竟是为什么？既然已经知道这种想法会造成恐惧，为什么我还要从苦与乐的角度思考过往和将来？难道思想就不可能从心理上停止吗？否则恐惧便永无尽头了。"

思想的运转方式之一，便是需要不停被占据。我们大多数人都希望自己的头脑一直被占据着，这样我们就不用去看真实的自己了。我们害怕内心的空白，害怕直视自己的恐惧。

在意识层面，你能发觉自己的恐惧，但在内心更深的层面上，你能觉察到它们吗？你如何才能发现那些潜藏的、隐秘的恐惧？恐惧究竟有没有显意识和潜意识之分？这是个非常重要的问题。专家、心

the psychologist, the analyst, have divided fear into deep and superficial layers, but if you follow what the psychologist says or what I say, you are understanding our theories, our dogmas, our knowledge, you are not understanding yourself. You cannot understand yourself according to Freud or Jung, or according to me. Other people's theories have no importance whatever. It is of yourself that you must ask the question, is fear to be divided into the conscious and subconscious? Or is there only fear which you translate into different forms? There is only one desire; there is only desire. You desire. The objects of desire change, but desire is always the same. So perhaps in the same way there is only fear. You are afraid of all sorts of things but there is only one fear.

When you realize that fear cannot be divided you will see that you have put away altogether this problem of the subconscious and so have cheated the psychologists and the analysts. When you understand that fear is a single movement which expresses itself in different ways and when you see the movement and not the object to which the movement goes, then you are facing an immense question: how can you look at it without the fragmentation which the mind has cultivated?

There is only total fear, but how can the mind which thinks in fragments observe this total picture? Can it? We have lived a life of fragmentation, and can look at that total fear only through the fragmentary process of thought. The whole process of the machinery of thinking is to break up everything into fragments: I love you and I hate you; you are my enemy, you are my friend; my peculiar idiosyncrasies and inclinations, my job, my position, my prestige, my wife, my child, my country and your country, my God and your God—all that is the fragmentation of thought. And this thought looks at the total state of fear, or tries to look at it, and

理学家和心理分析师，把恐惧划分为或深或浅的层面。但是，如果你听信了心理学家或者我所说的话，你就只是在理解我们的理论、教条和知识，而非在了解自我了。你不能遵照弗洛伊德、荣格或是我说的话来了解自己，他人的理论根本毫无价值。你要向你自己提出这个问题：恐惧究竟有没有显意识和潜意识之分？还是说只有一种恐惧，只是你把它诠释成了两种形式？只有一种欲望，有的只是欲望罢了——"你想要"。欲望的对象会变，但欲望本身始终如故。因此，或许恐惧也是如此：有的只是恐惧罢了。你害怕各种各样的东西，但恐惧只有一种。

当你意识到恐惧是不可分割的，你便会发现，你已经彻底抛开了潜意识这个问题，这个蒙蔽了心理学家与心理分析师的问题。当你懂得了所有的恐惧都属于同一种心理活动，只是以各种方式展现着自己，当你看清了那个活动，而非活动指向的对象，你便会迎来一个更大的问题：你如何才能面对它，却不受制于心智所培植的分割状态？

存在的只有整体的恐惧，但是以割裂的方式思考的心智，如何才能观察这整幅图景呢？它能观察吗？我们过着支离破碎的生活，只能透过支离破碎的思想过程去看整体的恐惧。这整个机械的思考过程就是要把一切都弄得分崩离析：我爱你，我恨你；你是我的敌人，你是我的朋友；我特殊的性情和倾向，我的工作，我的地位，我的威望，我的妻儿，我的国家和你的国家，我的上帝和你的上帝——这一切都是思想造成的破碎状态。正是这个思想看着恐惧的整体，或者试图去看，然后把它打成了碎片。因此我们发现，只有当思想活动不存在

reduces it to fragments. Therefore we see that the mind can look at this total fear only when there is no movement of thought.

Can you watch fear without any conclusion, without any interference of the knowledge you have accumulated about it? If you cannot, then what you are watching is the past, not fear; if you can, then you are watching fear for the first time without the interference of the past.

You can watch only when the mind is very quiet, just as you can listen to what someone is saying only when your mind is not chattering with itself, carrying on a dialogue with itself about its own problems and anxieties. Can you in the same way look at your fear without trying to resolve it, without bringing in its opposite, courage—actually look at it and not try to escape from it? When you say, "I must control it, I must get rid of it, I must understand it", you are trying to escape from it.

You can observe a cloud or a tree or the movement of a river with a fairly quiet mind because they are not very important to you, but to watch yourself is far more difficult because there the demands are so practical, the reactions so quick. So when you are directly in contact with fear or despair, loneliness or jealousy, or any other ugly state of mind, can you look at it so completely that your mind is quiet enough to see it?

Can the mind perceive fear and not the different forms of fear—perceive total fear, not what you are afraid of? If you look merely at the details of fear or try to deal with your fears one by one, you will never come to the central issue which is to learn to live with fear.

To live with a living thing such as fear requires a mind and heart that are extraordinarily subtle, that have no conclusion and can therefore follow every movement of fear. Then if you observe and live with it— and this doesn't take a whole day, it can take a minute or a second to know

时，心智才能去看恐惧的整体。

你能不能直视恐惧，不带有任何结论，也不让过往积累的知识横加干涉？如果不能，那么你看到的便是过去，而不是恐惧；如果你可以，那么你就第一次不受过去干涉地看到了恐惧本身。

唯有当内心异常平静时，你才能去看，就像只有当你的心没有喋喋不休，没有为自己的问题和焦虑自言自语时，你方能倾听别人所说的话。同样，你能不能正视自己的恐惧，不试图解决它，也不引入它的对立面——勇气，只是真切地看着它，而不试图逃避它？一旦你说："我必须控制它，我必须除掉它，我必须了解它"，你就是在设法逃避它。

你可以用一颗平静无波的心，观看一朵云、一棵树或是流动的河水，因为它们对你来说并不重要。但是观察你自己要困难多了，因为你的需求是如此实际，反应又是如此迅捷。因此，当你直截了当地接触恐惧或绝望，孤独或嫉妒，或是其他丑陋的心态，你能不能如此完整地注视它，乃至你的心平静得足以看清它？

心能否洞察恐惧，而非恐惧的各种形式——洞察整体的恐惧，而不是你害怕的对象？如果你只去看恐惧的细节，或是设法一个个地对付恐惧，那么你就永远无法直抵问题的核心，也就是学习如何与恐惧共处。

若要与一件活生生的东西共处，譬如恐惧，就需要头脑与内心都极为敏锐，没有任何结论，因而能够跟随恐惧的一举一动。如果你能观察并与之共处——这无须花费一整天的工夫，可能花一分钟或是

the whole nature of fear—if you live with it so completely you inevitably ask, "Who is the entity who is living with fear? Who is it who is observing fear, watching all the movements of the various forms of fear as well as being aware of the central fact of fear? Is the observer a dead entity, a static being, who has accumulated a lot of knowledge and information about himself, and is it that dead thing who is observing and living with the movement of fear? Is the observer the past or is he a living thing?" What is your answer? Do not answer me, answer yourself. Are you, the observer, a dead entity watching a living thing or are you a living thing watching a living thing? Because in the observer the two states exist.

The observer is the censor who does not want fear; the observer is the totality of all his experiences about fear. So the observer is separate from that thing he calls fear; there is space between them; he is forever trying to overcome it or escape from it and hence this constant battle between himself and fear—this battle which is such a waste of energy.

As you watch, you learn that the observer is merely a bundle of ideas and memories without any validity or substance, but that fear is an actuality and that you are trying to understand a fact with an abstraction which, of course, you cannot do. But, in fact, is the observer who says, "I am afraid", any different from the thing observed which is fear? The observer is fear and when that is realized there is no longer any dissipation of energy in the effort to get rid of fear, and the time-space interval between the observer and the observed disappears. When you see that you are a part of fear, not separate from it—that you are fear—then you cannot do anything about it; then fear comes totally to an end.

一秒钟即可洞悉恐惧的整个本质——如果你如此全然地与之共处，你必然会问："与恐惧共处的那个存在是谁？是谁在观察恐惧，注视着各种恐惧的所有活动，同时又能觉知恐惧这个核心事实？那个观察者是不是一个已死的、停滞的存在——他积累了关于自己的大量知识和信息——是不是那个僵死的东西在观察以及与恐惧的活动共处？那个观察者究竟是过去，还是一个活生生的东西？"你会如何作答？不要回答我，回答你自己。你，这个观察者，是一个在观察活物的僵死的存在，还是说，你是一个在观察活物的鲜活的存在？因为在观察者身上，可能存在这两种状态。

观察者就是那个不想要恐惧的审查官，就是他关于恐惧的所有经验的整体。因此观察者与他所谓恐惧分开了，二者之间有了距离。他一直设法克服或者逃避这个距离，于是他与恐惧之间征战不休，而这场战争是能量的严重浪费。

然而在观察当中，你会发现观察者不过是一团毫无价值或实质的观念和经验，而恐惧是鲜活的事实，你若试图用抽象的概念去了解事实，那当然是不可能的。事实上，那个说"我害怕"的观察者，与他所观察的恐惧有任何两样吗？观察者就是恐惧，当你领悟到这一点，就不会再因为努力除掉恐惧而耗费能量了，观察者与所观之物之间的时空隔阂也就消失了。当你看清你就是恐惧的一部分，你与它并无分别——你即是恐惧——你便不会再对它做什么了，此时恐惧也就彻底止息了。

PART 6
第六部分

Violence—Anger—Justification
and Condemnation—The Ideal and the
Actual

暴力——愤怒——辩解与谴责——
理想与事实

Fear, pleasure, sorrow, thought and violence are all interrelated. Most of us take pleasure in violence, in disliking somebody, hating a particular race or group of people, having antagonistic feelings towards others. But in a state of mind in which all violence has come to an end there is a joy which is very different from the pleasure of violence with its conflicts, hatreds and fears.

Can we go to the very root of violence and be free from it? Otherwise we shall live everlastingly in battle with each other. If that is the way you want to live—and apparently most people do—then carry on; if you say, "Well, I'm sorry, violence can never end", then you and I have no means of communication, you have blocked yourself; but if you say there might be a different way of living, then we shall be able to communicate with each other.

So let us consider together, those of us who can communicate, whether it is at all possible totally to end every form of violence in ourselves and still live in this monstrously brutal world. I think it is possible. I don't want to have a breath of hate, jealousy, anxiety or fear in me. I want to live completely at peace. Which doesn't mean that I want to die. I want to live on this marvellous earth, so full, so rich, so beautiful. I want to look at the trees, flowers, rivers, meadows, women, boys and girls, and at the same time live completely at peace with myself and with the world. What can I do?

恐惧、快感、悲伤、思想与暴力，都是密切相关的。我们大多数人都以暴力为乐，从讨厌某人、憎恨某个特定的种族或人群、敌视他人中取乐。然而，唯有在一切暴力都止息的心灵状态下，才会出现一种喜悦，它与从冲突、仇恨和恐惧等暴力中获得的快感截然不同。

我们能否直抵暴力的根本并从中解脱出来？否则我们就只能活在彼此之间永无休止的征战当中。倘若那是你想要的生活方式——显然大部分人正是如此——那就继续好了；如果你说："哦，很遗憾，暴力绝不可能终止"，那么你我之间的沟通便到此为止，你已经囚禁了自己。但是如果你说："或许存在另一种生活之道"，那么我们就可以继续交流了。

所以，我们当中可以交流的那些人，请一起来考虑一下：究竟有没有可能彻底终止自己身上的所有暴力，同时依然活在这个极其残酷的世界上？我认为这是可能的。我不想让自己身上有一丝仇恨、嫉妒、焦虑或恐惧的气息，我想完全和平地活着。这并不是说我想死掉。恰恰相反，我想活在如此丰盛、如此富饶、如此美丽的奇妙地球之上，饱览花草树木、河流原野、男女老幼，同时又与自己、与世界完全和平共处。那我该怎么办？

如果我们懂得如何观察暴力，不仅是外在社会中的暴力——战

If we know how to look at violence, not only outwardly in society—the wars, the riots, the national antagonisms and class conflicts—but also in ourselves, then perhaps we shall be able to go beyond it.

Here is a very complex problem. For centuries upon centuries man has been violent; religions have tried to tame him throughout the world and none of them have succeeded. So if we are going into the question we must, it seems to me, be at least very serious about it because it will lead us into quite a different domain, but if we want merely to play with the problem for intellectual entertainment we shall not get very far.

You may feel that you yourself are very serious about the problem but that as long as so many other people in the world are not serious and are not prepared to do anything about it, what is the good of your doing anything? I don't care whether they take it seriously or not. I take it seriously, that is enough. I am not my brother's keeper. I myself, as a human being, feel very strongly about this question of violence and I will see to it that in myself I am not violent—but I cannot tell you or anybody else, "Don't be violent." It has no meaning—unless you yourself want it. So if you yourself really want to understand this problem of violence let us continue on our journey of exploration together.

Is this problem of violence out there or here? Do you want to solve the problem in the outside world or are you questioning violence itself as it is in you? If you are free of violence in yourself the question is, "How am I to live in a world full of violence, acquisitiveness, greed, envy, brutality? Will I not be destroyed?" That is the inevitable question which is invariably asked. When you ask such a question it seems to me you are not actually living peacefully. If you live peacefully you will have no problem at all. You may be imprisoned because you refuse to join the army or shot because

争、暴乱、民族对抗与阶级纷争——还包括我们内心的暴力，那么或许我们就能超越它。

这是一个异常复杂的问题。数个世纪以来，人一直是暴力的，各派宗教都曾设法驯服全世界的人类，但没有一个成功过。因此，如果要深入探究这个问题，在我看来，我们就必须至少保持非常认真的态度，因为它将引我们走向一个截然不同的领域。但是，如果我们只是抱着智力消遣的玩闹心态对待这个问题，我们就无法走远。

你也许觉得自己对这个问题还是很认真的，但是，只要世上还有很多人不认真，而且也不打算为此有所行动，那么你的做法又于事何补呢？我才不在乎他们是否认真，我认真，这就够了。我可不是我兄弟的监护人。我自己，身为一个人，对于暴力这个问题有着强烈的感触，我会确保自己身上没有暴力，但我没法告诫你或是别人："别那么暴力。"那么做毫无意义，除非你自己希望不再暴力。因此，如果你自己真的想了解暴力这个问题，那就让我们一起继续我们的探索之旅。

暴力这个问题究竟是外在的还是内在的？你是想解决外在世界的这个问题，还是你在质问暴力这个问题本身，因为它就在你自己身上？如果你摆脱了自身的暴力，那么问题就成了："我该如何活在这个充斥着暴力、利欲、贪婪、羡妒与残暴的世界上？我难道不会被毁掉吗？"这是必定会被问到的一个无法回避的问题。如果你提出这样的问题，那么在我看来，你实际上并没有和平地活着。如果你和平地活着，你就根本不会有问题。你也许会被投入监狱，因为你拒绝入

you refuse to fight—but that is not a problem; you will be shot. It is extraordinarily important to understand this.

We are trying to understand violence as a fact, not as an idea, as a fact which exists in the human being, and the human being is myself. And to go into the problem I must be completely vulnerable, open, to it. I must expose myself to myself—not necessarily expose myself to you because you may not be interested—but I must be in a state of mind that demands to see this thing right to the end and at no point stops and says I will go no further.

Now it must be obvious to me that I am a violent human being. I have experienced violence in anger, violence in my sexual demands, violence in hatred, creating enmity, violence in jealousy and so on—I have experienced it, I have known it, and I say to myself, "I want to understand this whole problem not just one fragment of it expressed in war, but this aggression in man which also exists in the animals and of which I am a part."

Violence is not merely killing another. It is violence when we use a sharp word, when we make a gesture to brush away a person, when we obey because there is fear. So violence isn't merely organized butchery in the name of God, in the name of society or country. Violence is much more subtle, much deeper, and we are inquiring into the very depths of violence.

When you call yourself an Indian or a Muslim or a Christian or a European, or anything else, you are being violent. Do you see why it is violent? Because you are separating yourself from the rest of mankind. When you separate yourself by belief, by nationality, by tradition, it breeds violence. So a man who is seeking to understand violence does not belong to any country, to any religion, to any political party or partial system; he is

伍，或是被枪毙，因为你拒绝参战——你会被枪毙，但那并不是问题。理解这一点至关重要。

我们正试着了解暴力这个事实——并非概念，而是存在于一个人身上的事实，而这个人就是我自己。若要探究这个问题，我就必须彻底不设防，对它完全保持开放。我必须向自己完全敞开，不是向你暴露我自己——因为你可能不感兴趣——而是我必须处于这样的心智状态：渴望彻底看透这个问题，永不停步，绝不说我已到此为止。

我是一个暴力的人，这一点对我来说肯定是显而易见的。我经历过愤怒中的暴力，性欲、仇恨、敌意、嫉妒等当中的暴力。我经历过暴力，我熟悉暴力，于是我对自己说："我想弄清这整个问题，不单是它在战争中表现出的一个碎片，而是存在于我身为一分子的人类以及动物身上的这种侵略性。"

暴力并非仅仅是杀害他人，当我们使用尖刻的词语，做出蔑视他人的姿态，或是因为恐惧而顺从，这些都是暴力。所以暴力不仅仅是以上帝、以社会或国家之名进行的有组织的屠杀。暴力要微妙得多、深刻得多，而我们正在探究它更深的层面。

当你自称印度人、穆斯林、基督徒、欧洲人、或者无论什么人，你就是暴力的。你有没有发现为什么？因为你把自己与其他人割裂了开来。一旦你通过信仰、国籍、传统把自己割裂出来，你便酿成了暴力。因此，一个想真正了解暴力的人，不会属于任何国家、任何宗教、任何政党或是局部的体系，他关心的是对人类的彻底了解。

关于暴力，当今有两个主要的思想流派，一派认为："暴力是

concerned with the total understanding of mankind.

Now there are two primary schools of thought with regard to violence, one which says, "Violence is innate in man" and the other which says, "Violence is the result of the social and cultural heritage in which man lives." We are not concerned with which school we belong to—it is of no importance. What is important is the fact that we are violent, not the reason for it.

One of the most common expressions of violence is anger. When my wife or sister is attacked I say I am righteously angry; when my country is attacked, my ideas, my principles, my way of life, I am righteously angry. I am also angry when my habits are attacked or my petty little opinions. When you tread on my toes or insult me I get angry, or if you run away with my wife and I get jealous, that jealousy is called righteous because she is my property. And all this anger is morally justified. But to kill for my country is also justified. So when we are talking about anger, which is a part of violence, do we look at anger in terms of righteous and unrighteous anger according to our own inclinations and environmental drive, or do we see only anger? Is there righteous anger ever? Or is there only anger? There is no good influence or bad influence, only influence, but when you are influenced by something which doesn't suit me I call it an evil influence.

The moment you protect your family, your country, a bit of coloured rag called a flag, a belief, an idea, a dogma, the thing that you demand or that you hold, that very protection indicates anger. So can you look at anger without any explanation or justification, without saying, "I must protect my goods", or "I was right to be angry", or "How stupid of me to be angry"? Can you look at anger as if it were something by itself? Can you look at it completely objectively, which means neither defending it nor condemning

人的本性"，另一派则认为："暴力是人所处的社会与文化遗产的产物。"我们并不关心属于哪个流派，那根本不重要。重要的是"我们是暴力的"这个事实，而不是暴力的原因。

暴力最常见的表现形式之一便是愤怒。当我的妻子或姐妹受到侵犯，我说我有权义愤填膺；当我的国家、我的观点、我的原则或是生活方式受到了侵犯，我的愤怒也理直气壮。当我的习惯或是小小见解受到了攻击，我也会生气。如果你踩了我一脚或是侮辱了我，我会生气，或者，如果你带着我妻子私奔，我就会妒火中烧，那种嫉妒被认为是正当的，因为她是我的私有财产。所有这些愤怒都被道德认为是合理的，连为国杀敌都被认为是正当的。因此，当我们谈到愤怒，也就是暴力的一部分，我们是不是受自己的性情和环境所驱动，从正派与否的视角去看待愤怒的？还是说我们看到的只有愤怒本身？到底有没有正当的愤怒这回事？还是就只有愤怒罢了？影响根本没什么好坏之分，有的只是影响罢了。然而，当你受到了不合我意的影响，我就说那是邪恶的影响。

一旦你要保护自己的家庭、自己的国家、被称为"旗帜"的一小块彩色布条，保护某种信仰、某个观念、某套教条，保护你想要的或是抱持的东西，那种保护本身就包含了愤怒。所以，你能不能正视愤怒，却不做任何解释或辩护，不说"我必须保护自己的利益"或者"我生气是正当的"，也不说"我竟然生气了，我可真蠢"？你能不能看着愤怒，就好像愤怒是一个独立的存在？你能不能完全客观地看着它，既不维护也不谴责？你可以吗？

it? Can you?

Can I look at you if I am antagonistic to you or if I am thinking what a marvellous person you are? I can see you only when I look at you with a certain care in which neither of these things is involved. Now, can I look at anger in the same way, which means that I am vulnerable to the problem, I do not resist it, I am watching this extraordinary phenomenon without any reaction to it?

It is very difficult to look at anger dispassionately because it is a part of me, but that is what I am trying to do. Here I am, a violent human being, whether I am black, brown, white or purple. I am not concerned with whether I have inherited this violence or whether society has produced it in me; all I am concerned with is whether it is at all possible to be free from it. To be free from violence means everything to me. It is more important to me than sex, food, position, for this thing is corrupting me. It is destroying me and destroying the world, and I want to understand it, I want to be beyond it. I feel responsible for all this anger and violence in the world. I feel responsible—it isn't just a lot of words—and I say to myself, "I can do something only if I am beyond anger myself, beyond violence, beyond nationality". And this feeling I have that I must understand the violence in myself brings tremendous vitality and passion to find out.

But to be beyond violence I cannot suppress it, I cannot deny it, I cannot say, "Well, it is a part of me and that's that", or "I don't want it". I have to look at it, I have to study it, I must become very intimate with it and I cannot become intimate with it if I condemn it or justify it. We do condemn it, though; we do justify it. Therefore I am saying, stop for the time being condemning it or justifying it.

Now, if you want to stop violence, if you want to stop wars, how

　　如果我对你抱有敌意，或是觉得你为人很棒，那么我还能如实看待你吗？只有当我带着一种毫无成见的关怀去看你，我方能"看到"你。那么，我能不能以同样的方式去看待愤怒？也就是说，我能不能对那个问题毫不设防，不抗拒它，只是观察这个非同寻常的现象，却不做任何反应？

　　我们很难毫无偏见地去看愤怒，因为它就是我的一部分，但那确实是我尝试去做的。我就在这里，一个暴力的人，无论我肤色是黑是白，是棕是紫。我不关心这暴力是我遗传来的，还是社会在我身上植入的，我只关心究竟有没有可能摆脱它。从暴力中解脱，对我来说就是一切，它比性事、食物、地位都重要，因为这个东西在腐蚀着我。它正在毁掉我，毁掉这个世界，而我想了解它、超越它。我感到自己对世界上的一切愤怒和暴力都负有责任，我有这份责任感——这并非只是说辞——我告诉自己："唯有当我自己超越了愤怒、暴力和国家之分，我方能有所作为。""我必须了解自身暴力"的这份感受，便激发了探索真相的无穷活力和激情。

　　然而，若要超越暴力，我就不能压制它、否认它，我不能说："哦，它是我的一部分，那就这样吧"，也不能说："我不想要它"。我得去观察它、探究它，我必须与它亲密无间。若是我谴责它或是维护它，便无法与它亲密无间。可我们确实谴责它，或者维护它。于是我对自己说：暂且停止对它的谴责或是维护。

　　那么，你若想停止暴力、停止战争，你会为之付出多少精力、投入多少？你的孩子被杀，你儿子参军然后惨遭凌辱和屠杀，这些事对

much vitality, how much of yourself, do you give to it? Isn't it important to you that your children are killed, that your sons go into the army where they are bullied and butchered? Don't you care? My God, if that doesn't interest you, what does? Guarding your money? Having a good time? Taking drugs? Don't you see that this violence in yourself is destroying your children? Or do you see it only as some abstraction?

All right then, if you are interested, attend with all your heart and mind to find out. Don't just sit back and say, "Well, tell us all about it". I point out to you that you cannot look at anger nor at violence with eyes that condemn or justify and that if this violence is not a burning problem to you, you cannot put those two things away. So first you have to learn; you have to learn how to look at anger, how to look at your husband, your wife, your children; you have to listen to the politician, you have to learn why you are not objective, why you condemn or justify. You have to learn that you condemn and justify because it is part of the social structure you live in, your conditioning as a German or an Indian or a Negro or an American or whatever you happen to have been born, with all the dulling of the mind that this conditioning results in. To learn, to discover, something fundamental you must have the capacity to go deeply. If you have a blunt instrument, a dull instrument, you cannot go deeply. So what we are doing is sharpening the instrument, which is the mind—the mind which has been made dull by all this justifying and condemning. You can penetrate deeply only if your mind is as sharp as a needle and as strong as a diamond.

It is no good just sitting back and asking, "How am I to get such a mind?" You have to want it as you want your next meal, and to have it you must see that what makes your mind dull and stupid is this sense of invulnerability which has built walls round itself and which is part of this

你来说难道不重要吗？你难道不关心吗？我的天，如果那些你都不关心，你还关心什么？看紧你的钱财？寻欢作乐？吸食药物？你没发现你身上的这些暴力正在毁掉你的孩子吗？还是说你只把这当成是一个抽象的概念？

话说回来，如果你真的在意，那就付出你的全部身心去探明真相。不要只是袖手旁观地说："好吧，告诉我们到底是怎么回事。"我跟你说了，你不能用谴责或维护的眼光去看待愤怒或者暴力。如果暴力对你来说并不是一个迫在眉睫的问题，你是无法撇开谴责或辩解的。所以首先你必须学习，学习如何去看待愤怒，如何去看待你的丈夫、妻子、孩子，如何聆听政客；你必须了解你为何不客观，为何谴责或辩护。你必须了解，你之所以谴责和辩护，是因为那是你所处的社会结构的一部分，那是你身为一个德国人、印度人、黑人、美国人，或是无论你身为何人，所受的制约，正是这种制约严重钝化了心智。若要了解或发现某种根本的东西，你就必须具备深入探索的能力。如果你的工具迟钝、愚笨，你便无法深入。因此我们所做的正是磨快你的工具，也就是你的心智，它已经被这个辩护和谴责的过程钝化了。唯有当你的心智如钢针一样锋利、如钻石一样坚硬，你方能深深穿透下去。

只是袖手旁观地问："我如何才能拥有这样的心智？"这完全于事无补。你必须像渴望你的下一餐饭一样渴望它。若想拥有那样的心智，你就必须看清，令你的心迟钝愚蠢的，正是这种刀枪不入的防御，它在你四周筑起高墙，它就是谴责与辩解过程的一部分。如果心

condemnation and justification. If the mind can be rid of that, then you can look, study, penetrate, and perhaps come to a state that is totally aware of the whole problem.

So let us come back to the central issue—is it possible to eradicate violence in ourselves? It is a form of violence to say, "You haven't changed, why haven't you?" I am not doing that. It doesn't mean a thing to me to convince you of anything. It is your life, not my life. The way you live is your affair. I am asking whether it is possible for a human being living psychologically in any society to clear violence from himself inwardly? If it is, the very process will produce a different way of living in this world.

Most of us have accepted violence as a way of life. Two dreadful wars have taught us nothing except to build more and more barriers between human beings that is, between you and me. But for those of us who want to be rid of violence, how is it to be done? I do not think anything is going to be achieved through analysis, either by ourselves or by a professional. We might be able to modify ourselves slightly, live a little more quietly with a little more affection, but in itself it will not give total perception. But I must know how to analyse which means that in the process of analysis my mind becomes extraordinarily sharp, and it is that quality of sharpness, of attention, of seriousness, which will give total perception. One hasn't the eyes to see the whole thing at a glance; this clarity of the eye is possible only if one can see the details, then jump.

Some of us, in order to rid ourselves of violence, have used a concept, an ideal, called non-violence, and we think by having an ideal of the opposite to violence, non-violence, we can get rid of the fact, the actual— but we cannot. We have had ideals without number, all the sacred books are full of them, yet we are still violent—so why not deal with violence itself

智能够摆脱那些，你就可以观察、探究以及穿透了，或许就能达到一种全然了知这整个问题的境地。

因此，让我们回到这个核心问题上来——有没有可能根除我们身上的暴力？说"你没有改变，那你为什么还不改变？"这也是一种暴力的表现，我可没有这么做。说服你去做任何事，对我来说都没有丝毫意义。这是你的人生，不是我的，你的生活方式是你的事情。我问的是，一个人无论活在哪个社会上，他有没有可能彻底清除内心的暴力？如果可能，那么这个过程本身便会为世界造就一种截然不同的生活之道。

大多数人都接受了暴力就是我们的生活方式。两场可怕的战争什么都没有教会我们，除了在人与人之间，也就是你我之间筑造更多的藩篱。然而，对我们当中那些真的想要摆脱暴力的人来说，如何才能做到这一点？我认为，借助分析，无论是我们自己还是所谓专家的分析，都无法取得任何进展。我们或许可以稍微改善一下自己，拥有多一点关爱，活得稍微平静一点，但那并不会带来全然的洞察。但我必须知道如何分析，也就是说，在分析过程中，我的心变得极其敏锐，正是那份敏锐、关注和认真的品质会带来全然的洞察。一个人并没有一瞥即窥见全貌的眼光，只有当他能看清细节然后跨越，才可能拥有那样清澈的眼睛。

我们中的一些人，为了让自己摆脱暴力，运用了"非暴力"这个概念、这个理想，我们以为抱持与暴力相反的那个理想——"非暴力"，我们便能摆脱事实——但我们没有。我们怀揣不计其数的理

and forget the word altogether?

If you want to understand the actual you must give your whole attention, all your energy, to it. That attention and energy are distracted when you create a fictitious, ideal world. So can you completely banish the ideal? The man who is really serious, with the urge to find out what truth is, what love is, has no concept at all. He lives only in what is.

To investigate the fact of your own anger you must pass no judgement on it, for the moment you conceive of its opposite you condemn it and therefore you cannot see it as it is. When you say you dislike or hate someone that is a fact, although it sounds terrible. If you look at it, go into it completely, it ceases, but if you say, "I must not hate; I must have love in my heart", then you are living in a hypocritical world with double standards. To live completely, fully, in the moment is to live with what is, the actual, without any sense of condemnation or justification—then you understand it so totally that you are finished with it. When you see clearly the problem is solved.

But can you see the face of violence clearly—the face of violence not only outside you but inside you, which means that you are totally free from violence because you have not admitted ideology through which to get rid of it? This requires very deep meditation not just a verbal agreement or disagreement.

You have now read a series of statements but have you really understood? Your conditioned mind, your way of life, the whole structure of the society in which you live, prevent you from looking at a fact and being entirely free from it immediately. You say, "I will think about it; I will consider whether it is possible to be free from violence or not. I will try to be free." That is one of the most dreadful statements you can make, "I

想，所有的圣典都充斥着理想，可我们依然暴力，所以为什么不去应对暴力本身，把那个词彻底忘掉？

如果你想了解事实，就必须为它付出你全部的注意力、全部的能量。一旦你塑造出一个虚幻的、理想的世界，这份关注和能量便被耗散了。因此，你能否彻底摒弃理想？一个人若是真的认真，渴望发现何为真理、何为爱，他是绝不会抱有任何概念的，他只活在事实当中。

若要探究你自身愤怒的事实，你就决不能对它妄加评判，因为一旦你构想出它的对立面，你就已经谴责了它，进而无法如其所是地看到它。当你说你讨厌或是憎恨某个人，那便是事实，尽管听起来很吓人。如果你看着它，彻底地探究它，它就止息了。但是倘若你说："我决不能恨，我内心必须有爱"，你就活在了一个有着双重标准的虚伪的世界里。要在当下活得充分、完满，就要与事实、与真相共处，不做丝毫的谴责或辩解。只有此时你才能彻底地了解它，进而将它了结。当你彻底看清了，问题也就迎刃而解了。

但是，你能看清暴力的全貌吗？——既包括外在也包括你内心的暴力。那就意味着，你从暴力中完全解脱了出来，因为你不再允许借以清除暴力的理念涉入。这需要极深的冥想，而非仅仅从口头上表示同意与否。

到这里，你已经读到了一系列的说法，但你真的明白了吗？你受限的心智，你的生活方式，你所处的整个社会架构，都妨碍了你去直面事实，并即刻从中彻底解脱出来。你说："我会想一想，我会

will try". There is no trying, no doing your best. Either you do it or you don't do it. You are admitting time while the house is burning. The house is burning as a result of the violence throughout the world and in yourself and you say, "Let me think about it. Which ideology is best to put out the fire?" When the house is on fire, do you argue about the colour of the hair of the man who brings the water?

考虑有没有可能从暴力中解脱，我会努力获得自由的。""我会努力"——这是你所能说出的最糟糕的话了。根本就没有努力以及尽力而为这回事。你要么做，要么不做。房子已经着火了，你却在拖延时间。房子的失火，正是全世界以及你内心暴力的结果。你却说："我来想一想，用哪个理念灭火最好？"当房子正在熊熊燃烧，你还会争论取水救火的人究竟是何种发色吗？

PART 7
第七部分

Relationship—Conflict—Society
—Poverty—Drugs—Dependence
—Comparison—Desire—Ideals—
Hypocrisy

关系——冲突——社会——贫
穷——药物——依赖——比较——欲
望——理想——虚伪

The cessation of violence, which we have just been considering, does not necessarily mean a state of mind which is at peace with itself and therefore at peace in all its relationships.

Relationship between human beings is based on the image—forming, defensive mechanism. In all our relationships each one of us builds an image about the other and these two images have relationship, not the human beings themselves. The wife has an image about the husband—perhaps not consciously but nevertheless it is there—and the husband has an image about the wife. One has an image about one's country and about oneself, and we are always strengthening these images by adding more and more to them. And it is these images which have relationship. The actual relationship between two human beings or between many human beings completely end when there is the formation of images.

Relationship based on these images can obviously never bring about peace in the relationship because the images are fictitious and one cannot live in an abstraction. And yet that is what we are all doing: living in ideas, in theories, in symbols, in images which we have created about ourselves and others and which are not realities at all. All our relationships, whether they be with property, ideas or people, are based essentially on this image—forming, and hence there is always conflict.

How is it possible then to be completely at peace within ourselves and in all our relationships with others? After all, life is a movement in relationship,

我们之前所探讨的暴力的止息，并不一定会使你心境宁和，进而在所有关系中都能和平相处。

人与人之间的关系，奠基于塑造形象的防御机制之上。在所有关系中，我们每个人都在为他人塑造形象，进而是两个形象，而非两个真实的人之间产生了关系。妻子对丈夫抱有印象——也许不是有意识的，但印象确实存在——丈夫对妻子也抱有印象。一个人会对自己以及自己的国家抱有一个形象，我们也一直在添枝加叶地增强这些形象，而产生关系的正是这些形象。形象一旦树立起来，人与人之间的真实关系也就彻底终止了。

奠基于形象之上的关系，显然绝不可能为关系带来和平，因为形象是虚幻的，而人无法活在抽象的世界里。然而我们热衷于此：活在我们围绕自己和他人塑造的观念、理论、符号及形象当中——这些东西根本没有真实性可言。我们所有的关系，无论是与财产、与观念还是与他人的关系，基本上都奠基于形象塑造之上，因而冲突不断。

那么，我们如何才能内心平和，同时在所有关系中也能与他人和平共处？归根结底，生活即是关系中的互动，否则就根本没有生活可言。然而，如果生活奠基于抽象的概念或是臆想的假设之上，那么这种抽象的生活便必定会建立一种有如战场的关系。因此，一个人究竟

otherwise there is no life at all, and if that life is based on an abstraction, an idea, or a speculative assumption, then such abstract living must inevitably bring about a relationship which becomes a battlefield. So is it at all possible for man to live a completely orderly inward life without any form of compulsion, imitation, suppression or sublimation? Can he bring about such order within himself that it is a living quality not held within the framework of ideas—an inward tranquillity which knows no disturbance at any moment—not in some fantastic mythical abstract world but in the daily life of the home and the office?

I think we should go into this question very carefully because there is not one spot in our consciousness untouched by conflict. In all our relationships, whether with the most intimate person or with a neighbour or with society, this conflict exists—conflict being contradiction, a state of division, separation, a duality. Observing ourselves and our relationships to society we see that at all levels of our being there is conflict—minor or major conflict which brings about very superficial responses or devastating results.

Man has accepted conflict as an innate part of daily existence because he has accepted competition, jealousy, greed, acquisitiveness and aggression as a natural way of life. When we accept such a way of life we accept the structure of society as it is and live within the pattern of respectability. And that is what most of us are caught in because most of us want to be terribly respectable. When we examine our own minds and hearts, the way we think, the way we feel and how we act in our daily lives, we observe that as long as we conform to the pattern of society, life must be a battlefield. If we do not accept it—and no religious person can possibly accept such a society—then we will be completely free from the psychological structure of society.

Most of us are rich with the things of society. What society has created in us and what we have created in ourselves, are greed, envy, anger, hate, jealousy,

是否可能过一种内心井然有序的生活，没有丝毫强迫、仿效、压制或升华？他能不能在自己内心营造一份完全不受困于观念囹圄的鲜活秩序？并非在某个异想天开、抽象神秘的世界里，而是就在家庭与办公室的日常生活中，享有那份时刻都无波无澜的内心宁静。

我认为我们应当非常小心地探讨这个问题，因为我们的意识没有一处尚未被冲突所沾染。在我们所有的关系中，无论是与最亲近的人、与邻居还是与社会，这种冲突无所不在——冲突即是矛盾，一种分别、割裂、二元对立的状态。只要观察自己以及我们与社会的关系，便会发现，我们存在的所有层面上都满是冲突——大大小小的冲突引发了非常表层的反应或是灾难性的后果。

人接受了冲突是日常生活固有的一部分，因为他接受了竞争、嫉妒、贪婪、求取以及侵略是一种自然的生活方式。当我们接受了这样一种生活方式，我们就接受了现行的社会结构，然后在虚荣体面的框架下生活。我们多数人都深陷其中，因为我们都想过得极为体面。如果我们审视自己的头脑和内心，审视我们日常生活中的思维方式、感受方式和行为方式，便会发现，只要我们遵从社会的模式，生活便必定会成为战场。只有我们不接受这一点——真正的宗教人士是绝不可能接受这种社会的——我们才能彻底地从现行社会的心理结构中解脱出来。

我们大部分人身上都充满了社会的习气，社会在我们内心植入的，以及我们在自己身上营造的，是贪婪、羡慕、愤怒、仇恨、嫉妒和焦虑——这些品质在我们身上都非常丰富。全世界的各派宗教都在

anxiety—and with all these we are very rich. The various religions throughout the world have preached poverty. The monk assumes a robe, changes his name, shaves his head, enters a cell and takes a vow of poverty and chastity; in the East he has one loin cloth, one robe, one meal a day—and we all respect such poverty. But those men who have assumed the robe of poverty are still inwardly, psychologically, rich with the things of society because they are still seeking position and prestige; they belong to this order or that order, this religion or that religion; they still live in the divisions of a culture, a tradition. That is not poverty. Poverty is to be completely free of society, though one may have a few more clothes, a few more meals—good God, who cares? But unfortunately in most people there is this urge for exhibitionism.

Poverty becomes a marvellously beautiful thing when the mind is free of society. One must become poor inwardly for then there is no seeking, no asking, no desire, no - nothing! It is only this inward poverty that can see the truth of a life in which there is no conflict at all. Such a life is a benediction not to be found in any church or any temple.

How is it possible then to free ourselves from the psychological structure of society, which is to free ourselves from the essence of conflict? It is not difficult to trim and lop off certain branches of conflict, but we are asking ourselves whether it is possible to live in complete inward and therefore outward tranquillity? Which does not mean that we shall vegetate or stagnate. On the contrary, we shall become dynamic, vital, full of energy.

To understand and to be free of any problem we need a great deal of passionate and sustained energy, not only physical and intellectual energy but an energy that is not dependent on any motive, any psychological stimulus or drug. If we are dependent on any stimulus that very stimulus makes the mind dull and insensitive. By taking some form of drug we may

宣扬清贫的生活。修道士披上僧袍，更名改姓，剃度出家，藏身斗室，宣誓安贫守贞；到东方则是一块腰布、一条长袍、一日一餐——我们都尊崇这样清贫的生活。但是这些披上了清贫外衣的人，内心依然充斥着社会的习性，因为他们依然追求着地位与权势；他们属于这个或那个社团、这派或那派宗教；他们依旧活在文化与传统的分别当中。这根本不是真正的清贫。真正的清贫是彻底从社会中解脱出来，哪怕有多几件衣服、吃多几餐饭——我的天，谁在乎这些呢？但不幸的是，大部分人都爱出这种风头。

唯有心灵摆脱了社会的束缚，清贫方能成为一件美妙无比的事。一个人必须内心变得清贫，此时他才不再追寻，不再需索，不再要求——也就是一无所求！拥有了内在的清贫，方能窥见那毫无冲突的生活的真面目。这样的生活是一种无法在任何教堂、任何寺庙中找到的至福。

那么，要怎样才能把我们自己从社会的心理结构中解放出来，也就是摆脱冲突的根本？修剪、砍掉冲突的某些枝丫并不困难，但我们问自己的是，生活中是否可能拥有内心的全然宁静，进而拥有外在的宁静？这并不意味着我们活得呆板凝滞、无所事事。恰恰相反，我们将会变得生气勃勃、充满活力。

若要了解并消除任何一个问题，我们都需要巨大的热情以及源源不断的活力，不单单是身体和头脑的活力，而是一股不依赖于任何动机、任何心理刺激或是药物的活力。只要我们依赖任何一种刺激，那个刺激物本身便会令心智变得麻木、迟钝。通过吸食药物，我们也许

find enough energy temporarily to see things very clearly but we revert to our former state and therefore become dependent on that drug more and more. So all stimulation, whether of the church or of alcohol or of drugs or of the written or spoken word, will inevitably bring about dependence, and that dependence prevents us from seeing clearly for ourselves and therefore from having vital energy.

We all unfortunately depend psychologically on something. Why do we depend? Why is there this urge to depend? We are taking this journey together; you are not waiting for me to tell you the causes of your dependence. If we enquire together we will both discover and therefore that discovery will be your own, and hence, being yours, it will give you vitality.

I discover for myself that I depend on something—an audience, say, which will stimulate me. I derive from that audience, from addressing a large group of people, a kind of energy. And therefore I depend on that audience, on those people, whether they agree or disagree. The more they disagree the more vitality they give me. If they agree it becomes a very shallow, empty thing. So I discover that I need an audience because it is a very stimulating thing to address people. Now why? Why do I depend? Because in myself I am shallow, in myself I have nothing, in myself I have no source which is always full and rich, vital, moving, living. So I depend. I have discovered the cause.

But will the discovery of the cause free me from being dependent? The discovery of the cause is merely intellectual, so obviously it does not free the mind from its dependency. The mere intellectual acceptance of an idea, or the emotional acquiescence in an ideology, cannot free the mind from being dependent on something which will give it stimulation. What frees the mind from dependence is seeing the whole structure and nature of stimulation and dependence and how that dependence makes the mind

能暂时找到充足的能量来看清事物，但很快便会恢复原状，进而会越来越依赖那种药物。因此所有的刺激，无论来自教堂、酒精、药物，还是来自语言、文字，都不可避免地会造成依赖，妨碍我们亲自看清真相，进而损害我们的生命力。

不幸的是，我们心理上都有所依赖。我们为何依赖？为何会有这种依赖的冲动？我们是在一起踏上这段旅程，你不要等我来告诉你依赖的原因。如果我们是在一起探索，我们双方都去发现真相，那么那个发现就是你自己的，因此会带给你充沛的活力。

我发现自己有所依赖，比如说，我依赖听众，他们会激励我。我从那群听众，从给一大群人讲话当中获得了某种能量。因此我依赖那些听众、依赖那群人，无论他们是否赞同我。他们越是不赞同，带给我的活力就越多。如果他们都赞同，反而变成了一件非常肤浅、非常空洞的事。所以我发现我需要听众，因为当众演说是一件非常刺激的事。那是为什么？我为何依赖？因为我内心空洞、一无所有，内心没有那始终完满、富足、流动、鲜活与生机勃勃的源头，所以才会依赖。我发现了依赖的原因。

然而，发现了原因便能让我从依赖中解脱吗？发现原因不过是道理上明白了，因此显然不会让心智摆脱依赖。仅仅从思想上接受一个观点，或是从情感上认同一个理念，是无法让心智从提供刺激的依赖中解脱的。让心解脱的，是看清刺激和依赖的整个结构与本质，看清那份依赖是如何令心智愚蠢、迟钝以及了无生气的。看清问题的全貌，即可让心解脱。

stupid, dull and inactive. Seeing the totality of it alone frees the mind.

So I must enquire into what it means to see totally. As long as I am looking at life from a particular point of view or from a particular experience I have cherished, or from some particular knowledge I have gathered, which is my background, which is the "me", I cannot see totally. I have discovered intellectually, verbally, through analysis, the cause of my dependence, but whatever thought investigates must inevitably be fragmentary, so I can see the totality of something only when thought does not interfere.

Then I see the fact of my dependence; I see actually what is. I see it without any like or dislike; I do not want to get rid of that dependence or to be free from the cause of it. I observe it, and when there is observation of this kind I see the whole picture, not a fragment of the picture, and when the mind sees the whole picture there is freedom. Now I have discovered that there is a dissipation of energy when there is fragmentation. I have found the very source of the dissipation of energy.

You may think there is no waste of energy if you imitate, if you accept authority, if you depend on the priest, the ritual, the dogma, the party or on some ideology, but the following and acceptance of an ideology, whether it is good or bad, whether it is holy or unholy, is a fragmentary activity and therefore a cause of conflict, and conflict will inevitably arise so long as there is a division between "what should be" and "what is", and any conflict is a dissipation of energy.

If you put the question to yourself, "How am I to be free from conflict?", you are creating another problem and hence you are increasing conflict, whereas if you just see it as a fact—see it as you would see some concrete object—clearly, directly—then you will understand essentially the truth of a life in which there is no conflict at all.

所以我必须探究"看清整体"意味着什么。只要我还在从某个特定的视角，从我珍视的某次经验，或是从我积攒的某些知识——那就是我的背景，那就是"我"——去看待人生，我就无法看清整体。借助分析，我从道理上、字面上找到了依赖的原因，但无论思想探究什么，都必定是支离破碎的。因此，只有当思想不再干涉时，我方能看清事物的整体。

于是我看到了自己依赖的真相，我真切地看到了"现实"。我看着它，不带好恶，既不想克服依赖，也不想摆脱依赖的原因。我只是观察它，唯有这样观察时，我方能见到整幅图景，而非一个片段。当心智见到了全貌，自由便来临了。同时我发现，只要支离破碎还在，便会耗费能量。我找到了能量耗费的源头。

你或许以为，如果你效仿他人，如果你接受权威，如果你依赖牧师、仪式、教条、党派或者意识形态，那并不会耗费你的能量。但实际上，对任何一种意识形态的追随与接受，无论好坏，无论神圣与否，都是支离破碎的行为，因而必定会导致冲突。只要"应当如何"与"现在如何"之间存在分别，冲突便在所难免，而任何冲突都是能量的浪费。

如果你问自己："我如何才能摆脱冲突？"，你便制造了另一个问题，因而加剧了冲突。反之，如果你清晰地、直截了当地、如实地看到它——就好像你看到了一个具体的物件——你便可以从根本上领悟了无冲突的生命真相。

让我们换个角度来说明：我们总是把自己"实际如何"与"应当

Let us put it another way. We are always comparing what we are with what we should be. The should-be is a projection of what we think we ought to be. Contradiction exists when there is comparison, not only with something or somebody, but with what you were yesterday, and hence there is conflict between what has been and what is. There is what is only when there is no comparison at all, and to live with what is, is to be peaceful. Then you can give your whole attention without any distraction to what is within yourself—whether it be despair, ugliness, brutality, fear, anxiety, loneliness—and live with it completely; then there is no contradiction and hence no conflict.

But all the time we are comparing ourselves—with those who are richer or more brilliant, more intellectual, more affectionate, more famous, more this and more that. The "more" plays an extraordinarily important part in our lives; this measuring ourselves all the time against something or someone is one of the primary causes of conflict.

Now why is there any comparison at all? Why do you compare yourself with another? This comparison has been taught from childhood. In every school A is compared with B, and A destroys himself in order to be like B. When you do not compare at all, when there is no ideal, no opposite, no factor of duality, when you no longer struggle to be different from what you are— what has happened to your mind? Your mind has ceased to create the opposite and has become highly intelligent, highly sensitive, capable of immense passion, because effort is a dissipation of passion—passion which is vital energy—and you cannot do anything without passion.

If you do not compare yourself with another you will be what you are. Through comparison you hope to evolve, to grow, to become more intelligent, more beautiful. But will you? The fact is what you are, and by comparing you are fragmenting the fact which is a waste of energy. To

如何"做比较，"应当如何"即我们所勾勒的自己应该成为的样子。而只要进行比较，矛盾就必定存在，你不只与某人、某事，还与昨天的你比较，因而"已然如何"与"现在如何"便产生了冲突。比较根本不存在时，"现在如何"才能呈现，与"现在如何"共处，方能平和宁静。此时你便能毫无扭曲地全神贯注于自己内心的现实——无论是绝望、丑陋、残酷、恐惧、焦虑，还是孤寂——并与之全然共处；此时矛盾将不复存在，冲突也随即止息。

然而，我们总是拿自己跟别人比较——那些人更富有、更聪明、更渊博、更有爱、更有名、更加如此这般。"更加"在我们的生活中起着极端重要的作用，而这种不停拿某人、某事来衡量自己的做法，便是冲突的主要肇因之一。

那么，究竟为何要比较？你为何要与人相比？我们从小就受到了这样的教育。每所学校都拿甲跟乙来比，为了成为乙，甲便要抹杀自己。而当你根本不比较，根本不抱任何理想、任何对立面以及二元性的因素，当你不再努力变得与真实的自己不同，你的心会怎样？你的心停止了塑造对立面，已然变得高度智慧、高度敏锐，具备了无限的激情，因为努力会损耗激情。激情即是生命力，若没有了它，你寸步难行。

如果你不把自己与他人比较，你便可以做真实的自己。通过比较，你希望进步、成长，希望变得更加睿智、更加美丽。可是你会吗？你实际的样子才是事实，比较则令你割裂了事实，耗费了能量。毫无比较地看到真实的自己，会赋予你惊人的能量去观察。当你能够

see what you actually are without any comparison gives you tremendous energy to look. When you can look at yourself without comparison you are beyond comparison, which does not mean that the mind is stagnant with contentment. So we see in essence how the mind wastes energy which is so necessary to understand the totality of life.

I don't want to know with whom I am in conflict; I don't want to know the peripheral conflicts of my being. What I want to know is why conflict should exist at all. When I put that question to myself I see a fundamental issue which has nothing to do with peripheral conflicts and their solutions. I am concerned with the central issue and I see—perhaps you see also? —that the very nature of desire, if not properly understood, must inevitably lead to conflict.

Desire is always in contradiction. I desire contradictory things—which doesn't mean that I must destroy desire, suppress, control or sublimate it—I simply see that desire itself is contradictory. It is not the objects of desire but the very nature of desire which is contradictory. And I have to understand the nature of desire before I can understand conflict. In ourselves we are in a state of contradiction, and that state of contradiction is brought about by desire—desire being the pursuit of pleasure and the avoidance of pain, which we have already been into.

So we see desire as the root of all contradiction—wanting something and not wanting it—a dual activity. When we do something pleasurable there is no effort involved at all, is there? But pleasure brings pain and then there is a struggle to avoid the pain, and that again is a dissipation of energy. Why do we have duality at all? There is, of course, duality in nature—man and woman, light and shade, night and day—but inwardly, psychologically, why do we have duality?

正视自己而不做比较，你便超越了比较——但这并不意味着心因满足而停滞不前。因此，我们从根本上看清了心是如何耗费能量的，那能量本是了解人生的整体所不可或缺的。

我并不想了解我与谁有冲突，也不想了解我生活中那些外围的冲突，我只想了解冲突究竟为何存在。当我向自己提出这个问题，我就发现了一个重大课题，而它与外围的冲突及其解决之道毫无关系。我关心的是核心问题，而且我发现——或许你也发现了——欲望的本质，倘若没有得到恰当的了解，就必定会导致冲突。

欲望总是矛盾重重。我想要的东西相互矛盾——并不是说我必须熄灭欲望，也不是要压抑、控制或者升华它——我只是发现欲望本身是自相矛盾的。并不是说欲望的对象互相矛盾，而是欲望的本性即是矛盾的。在能对冲突有所了解之前，我必须首先了解欲望的本质。我们自身便处于矛盾状态当中，而那种矛盾状态正是由欲望所引发的——欲望即是趋乐避苦，这一点我们之前已经探讨过了。

因此，我们发现欲望即是一切矛盾的根源——想要又不想要——这样一种二元分裂的行为。我们在做一件愉快的事时，是丝毫不用费力的，对吗？但快感会招来痛苦，随后你便会努力避开痛苦，而那又会耗费能量。我们内心究竟为何会有二元对立？毫无疑问，自然界中是存在二元性的——男人和女人，光与影，昼与夜——但是内在、心理上，我们为何会有二元对立？

请和我一起思考这个问题，不要等我来告诉你答案，你得开动自己的脑筋去搞清楚。我的话只是一面供你观察自己的镜子。我们为何

Please think this out with me, don't wait for me to tell you. You have to exercise your own mind to find out. My words are merely a mirror in which to observe yourself. Why do we have this psychological duality? Is it that we have been brought up always to compare "what is" with "what should be"? We have been conditioned in what is right and what is wrong, what is good and what is bad, what is moral and what is immoral. Has this duality come into being because we believe that thinking about the opposite of violence, the opposite of envy, of jealousy, of meanness, will help us to get rid of those things? Do we use the opposite as a lever to get rid of what is? Or is it an escape from the actual?

Do you use the opposite as a means of avoiding the actual which you don't know how to deal with? Or is it because you have been told by thousands of years of propaganda that you must have an ideal - the opposite of "what is" —in order to cope with the present? When you have an ideal you think it helps you to get rid of "what is", but it never does. You may preach non-violence for the rest of your life and all the time be sowing the seeds of violence.

You have a concept of what you should be and how you should act, and all the time you are in fact acting quite differently; so you see that principles, beliefs and ideals must inevitably lead to hypocrisy and a dishonest life. It is the ideal that creates the opposite to what is, so if you know how to be with "what is", then the opposite is not necessary.

Trying to become like somebody else, or like your ideal, is one of the main causes of contradiction, confusion and conflict. A mind that is confused, whatever it does, at any level, will remain confused; any action born of confusion leads to further confusion. I see this very clearly; I see it as clearly as I see an immediate physical danger. So what happens? I cease to act in terms of confusion any more. Therefore inaction is complete action.

会有这种心理上的二元对立？是不是因为我们从小所受的教育就是拿"现在如何"与"应当如何"相比？我们被局限在了"何为对""何为错""何为好""何为坏""何为道德""何为不道德"这些观念当中。这种二元性之所以形成，是不是因为我们以为想着暴力、羡慕、嫉妒、卑鄙的反面，便会帮我们去除这些东西？我们是不是把对立面当作了去除"现实"的杠杆？还是说，那其实只是对事实的逃避？

你是否把对立面当成了一种工具，用来逃避你不知如何应对的事实？抑或，是不是因为几千年来的洗脑，都在告诉你必须怀揣理想——"现实"的反面——来应对当下？你怀揣理想，以为它能帮你去除"现实"，但它从未做到。你或许余生都在祈祷非暴力，可同时又一直在播种暴力。

你抱持"你应当如何"以及"你该如何为人处世"的理念，可实际上你的行为一直大相径庭。因此你发现，原则、信仰和理想必定会导致虚伪以及不诚实的生活。正是理想造就了现实的对立面，因此，倘若你知道如何与"现实"共处，对立面便没有了存在的必要。

总想变成别人或是理想的样子，是造成矛盾、困惑与冲突的主因之一。一颗困惑的心，无论它做什么，也无论属于哪个层面，都始终是困惑的，而脱胎于困惑的行为必将导致进一步的困惑。我非常清晰地看到了这一点，就像看到了身体上迫在眉睫的危险，然后会怎样？我彻底停止了困惑的行为，因此安然不动即是完满的行动。

PART 8

第八部分

Freedom—Revolt—Solitude—
Innocence—Living with Ourselves as
We Are

自由——反叛——独处——纯
真——与真实的自己共处

None of the agonies of suppression, nor the brutal discipline of conforming to a pattern has led to truth. To come upon truth the mind must be completely free, without a spot of distortion.

But first let us ask ourselves if we really want to be free? When we talk of freedom are we talking of complete freedom or of freedom from some inconvenient or unpleasant or undesirable thing? We would like to be free from painful and ugly memories and unhappy experiences but keep our pleasurable, satisfying ideologies, formulas and relationships. But to keep the one without the other is impossible, for, as we have seen, pleasure is inseparable from pain.

So it is for each one of us to decide whether or not we want to be completely free. If we say we do, then we must understand the nature and structure of freedom.

Is it freedom when you are free from something—free from pain, free from some kind of anxiety? Or is freedom itself something entirely different? You can be free from jealousy, say, but isn't that freedom a reaction and therefore not freedom at all? You can be free from dogma very easily, by analysing it, by kicking it out, but the motive for that freedom from dogma has its own reaction because the desire to be free from a dogma may be that it is no longer fashionable or convenient. Or you can be free from nationalism because you believe in internationalism or because you feel it is no longer economically necessary to cling to this silly

痛苦的自我压制，谨遵模式的残酷戒律，都无法通往真理。若要邂逅真理，心就必须全然自由，没有半点扭曲。

但是我们首先来问问自己：我们真的想要自由吗？我们所说的"自由"，究竟是指彻底的自由呢，抑或只是摆脱某些不方便、不愉快、不想要的东西罢了？我们希望摆脱痛苦、丑陋的记忆与不快的经验，但保留那些愉快的、令人满足的理念、模式和关系。但只留其中之一是不可能的，因为正如我们所见，快乐与痛苦是密不可分的。

因此，我们每个人都需要决定自己究竟想不想要彻底的自由。如果想要，那么我们就必须了解自由的本质与结构。

当你从某种东西中解脱出来——比如，摆脱了痛苦或者某种焦虑，那是自由吗？抑或自由本身是一种截然不同的东西？比如说，你也许能摆脱嫉妒，但那种解脱不正是一种反应吗？因而根本算不上自由。通过分析或者剔除，你可以轻易地摆脱教条，但摆脱教条的动机本身即会带来反应，因为想要摆脱教条的愿望，可能源于它已不再时髦或是不再便利。又或者你可以摆脱国家主义，因为你开始信奉国际主义，或者因为你觉得从经济角度来看，已经没必要再抱守着愚不可及的民族主义教条、旗帜等诸如此类的鬼话。你可以轻松地摒弃这些。又或者，你可以反对某些精神领袖或政治领袖，他们原本承诺你

nationalistic dogma with its flag and all that rubbish. You can easily put that away. Or you may react against some spiritual or political leader who has promised you freedom as a result of discipline or revolt. But has such rationalism, such logical conclusion, anything to do with freedom?

If you say you are free from something, it is a reaction which will then become another reaction which will bring about another conformity, another form of domination. In this way you can have a chain of reactions and accept each reaction as freedom. But it is not freedom; it is merely a continuity of a modified past which the mind clings to.

The youth of today, like all youth, are in revolt against society, and that is a good thing in itself, but revolt is not freedom because when you revolt it is a reaction and that reaction sets up its own pattern and you get caught in that pattern. You think it is something new. It is not; it is the old in a different mould. Any social or political revolt will inevitably revert to the good old bourgeois mentality.

Freedom comes only when you see and act, never through revolt. The seeing is the acting and such action is as instantaneous as when you see danger. Then there is no cerebration, no discussion or hesitation; the danger itself compels the act, and therefore to see is to act and to be free.

Freedom is a state of mind - not freedom from something but a sense of freedom, a freedom to doubt and question everything and therefore so intense, active and vigorous that it throws away every form of dependence, slavery, conformity and acceptance. Such freedom implies being completely alone. But can the mind brought up in a culture so dependent on environment and its own tendencies ever find that freedom which is complete solitude and in which there is no leadership, no tradition and no authority?

This solitude is an inward state of mind which is not dependent on

只要修炼或是反叛即可收获自由。但是，这样的理性主义，这样的逻辑推论，与自由有丝毫干系吗？

如果你说你从什么中解脱了，那不过是一种反应罢了，随后会带来另一种反应，引发另一种遵从、另一种控制。这样一来，你便产生了一连串的连锁反应，却把每次反应都当成了自由。但那根本不是自由，那只不过是心智所执着的过去在改头换面后的延续。

如今的年轻人，就像所有时代的年轻人一样反叛社会。这本身是件好事，但反叛并非自由，因为当你反叛，那不过是一种反应罢了，那种反应会设定自身的模式，然后你便困在其中。你以为那是什么新东西，但实际上不是；那只是新瓶装旧酒罢了。社会上或者政治上的任何反叛，都必定会原封不动地退回到旧有的资产阶级心态。

反叛绝不会带来自由，只有当你看清真相并付诸行动，自由才会到来。看清即是行动，这样的行动是刻不容缓的，就如同你目睹了危险，不经思忖、不经讨论或犹疑，危险本身便激发了行动。因此看清便是行动，便是自由。

自由是一种心灵状态——并非从什么中解脱，而是一份自由感，一种怀疑并质询一切的自由，它因而非常热烈、非常活跃以及生机勃勃，乃至能够将各种依赖、奴役、遵从以及接受彻底丢弃。这样的自由即意味着彻底孑然一身。然而，在如此依赖于环境及自身性情的文化当中成长起来的心灵，究竟能否找到那份孑然独处而又全无向导、传统和权威的自由？

这份独自即是这样一种内心状态——心不依赖于任何刺激、任

any stimulus or any knowledge and is not the result of any experience or conclusion. Most of us, inwardly, are never alone. There is a difference between isolation, cutting oneself off, and aloneness, solitude. We all know what it is to be isolated—building a wall around oneself in order never to be hurt, never to be vulnerable, or cultivating detachment which is another form of agony, or living in some dreamy ivory tower of ideology. Aloneness is something quite different.

You are never alone because you are full of all the memories, all the conditioning, all the mutterings of yesterday; your mind is never clear of all the rubbish it has accumulated. To be alone you must die to the past. When you are alone, totally alone, not belonging to any family, any nation, any culture, any particular continent, there is that sense of being an outsider. The man who is completely alone in this way is innocent and it is this innocency that frees the mind from sorrow.

We carry about with us the burden of what thousands of people have said and the memories of all our misfortunes. To abandon all that totally is to be alone, and the mind that is alone is not only innocent but young—not in time or age, but young, innocent, alive at whatever age—and only such a mind can see that which is truth and that which is not measurable by words.

In this solitude you will begin to understand the necessity of living with yourself as you are, not as you think you should be or as you have been. See if you can look at yourself without any tremor, any false modesty, any fear, any justification or condemnation—just live with yourself as you actually are.

It is only when you live with something intimately that you begin to understand it. But the moment you get used to it—get used to your own anxiety or envy or whatever it is—you are no longer living with it. If you live by a river, after a few days you do not hear the sound of the water any

何知识，也并非任何经验或结论的产物。我们大多数人的内心从未真正独处。独自、独处与孤立、隔绝自己是两回事。我们都知道隔绝是怎么回事：在四周建造围墙，以期刀枪不入，绝不受伤，或者培养超脱——而那是另一种痛苦——或是活在某座虚无缥缈的意识形态的象牙塔里。独处与之有着天壤之别。

你从未真正独处，因为你内心载满了昨日所有的记忆、所有的局限、所有的喋喋不休；你的心从未清空它积攒的所有垃圾。若要独处，你就必须对过往死去。当你独处，真的孑然一身，不隶属于任何家庭、任何民族、任何文化或是任何一个大洲，你就有了那份身为局外人的感觉。如此孑然独立的人才是纯真的，唯有这份纯真方能令心从悲伤中解脱。

我们身上背着沉重的包袱——成千上万人说过的话以及我们所有不幸的记忆。若想彻底摒弃这一切，便要孑然独立。这样的一颗心既天真又年轻——无关岁月与年纪，而是无论年纪大小都青春无邪、充满活力——唯有这样的一颗心方能洞见真理，领会那言语无法度量之物。

在独处中，你开始懂得需要与真实的自己共处，而非你认为自己应当如何或是已然如何。看看你能否正视自己，没有丝毫战栗，没有半点伪装的谦虚，没有任何恐惧、任何辩解或是非难，而只是与真实的自己共处。

唯有与某样东西亲密共处，你才能开始了解它。一旦你对它习以为常——对你自己的焦虑、羡妒或无论什么习以为常——你便不再与它共处了。如果你住在河边，几天之后便对水声听而不闻；抑或房间

more, or if you have a picture in the room which you see every day you lose it after a week. It is the same with the mountains, the valleys, the trees—the same with your family, your husband, your wife. But to live with something like jealousy, envy or anxiety you must never get used to it, never accept it. You must care for it as you would care for a newly planted tree, protect it against the sun, against the storm. You must care for it, not condemn it or justify it. Therefore you begin to love it. When you care for it, you are beginning to love it. It is not that you love being envious or anxious, as so many people do, but rather that you care for watching.

So can you—can you and I—live with what we actually are, knowing ourselves to be dull, envious, fearful, believing we have tremendous affection when we have not, getting easily hurt, easily flattered and bored - can we live with all that, neither accepting it nor denying it, but just observing it without becoming morbid, depressed or elated?

Now let us ask ourselves a further question. Is this freedom, this solitude, this coming into contact with the whole structure of what we are in ourselves—is it to be come upon through time? That is, is freedom to be achieved through a gradual process? Obviously not, because as soon as you introduce time you are enslaving yourself more and more. You cannot become free gradually. It is not a matter of time.

The next question is, can you become conscious of that freedom? If you say, "I am free", then you are not free. It is like a man saying, "I am happy". The moment he says, "I am happy" he is living in a memory of something that has gone. Freedom can only come about naturally, not through wishing, wanting, longing. Nor will you find it by creating an image of what you think it is. To come upon it the mind has to learn to look at life, which is a vast movement, without the bondage of time, for freedom lies beyond the field of consciousness.

里挂了幅画，你天天可以看到，一周之后你便对它视而不见。与群山、深谷、树木共处是同样的情形，与你的家人、丈夫、妻子共处，也是如此。然而，要与嫉妒、羡慕或是焦虑之类的东西共处，你也决不能习以为常，决不能接受它们。你必须关怀它，就像照料一棵新栽的树苗，保护它免遭烈日曝晒、骤雨侵袭。你必须照料它，既不谴责也不维护，于是你逐渐爱上了它。当你照料它，你就开始爱上它了。并不是说你要热衷于羡慕或是焦虑，就像很多人那样，而是你要乐于观察。

因此，你——你和我——能否与我们真实的自己共处？知道自己迟钝、羡妒、恐惧，内心无爱却自以为大爱无边，而且容易受伤、受宠若惊以及感觉无聊，我们能否与这一切共处，既不接受也不拒绝，只是如实观察，既不会变得病态、沮丧，也不会扬扬得意？

现在我们来问自己一个更为深入的问题：这份自由，这份单独，还有对我们真实内心全部构造的触动——这些要假以时日来达到吗？也就是说，自由需要经历一个渐进的过程才能实现吗？显然不是，因为一旦引入了时间，你便是在越来越深地奴役自己。你无法逐渐变得自由，这根本不是一个时间问题。

接下来的问题便是：你能意识到那份自由吗？倘若你说："我自由了"，那你就尚未自由。就像一个人说"我很快乐"，他说"我很快乐"的那一刻，就已经活在了对过往的回忆中。自由只能自然而然地到来，而非通过祈祷、需求或渴望。通过树立一个你理想中自由的样子，也无法找到它。若要邂逅自由，心就必须学会观察生活——生活是一场广袤的运动，不为时间所围限，因为自由在意识的领地之外。

PART 9
第九部分

Time—Sorrow—Death

时间——悲伤——死亡

I am tempted to repeat a story about a great disciple going to God and demanding to be taught truth. This poor God says, "My friend, it is such a hot day, please get me a glass of water." So the disciple goes out and knocks on the door of the first house he comes to and a beautiful young lady opens the door. The disciple falls in love with her and they marry and have several children. Then one day it begins to rain, and keeps on raining, raining, raining—the torrents are swollen, the streets are full, the houses are being washed away. The disciple holds on to his wife and carries his children on his shoulders and as he is being swept away he calls out, "Lord, please save me", and the Lord says, "Where is that glass of water I asked for?"

It is rather a good story because most of us think in terms of time. Man lives by time. Inventing the future has been a favourite game of escape.

We think that changes in ourselves can come about in time, that order in ourselves can be built up little by little, added to day by day. But time doesn't bring order or peace, so we must stop thinking in terms of gradualness. This means that there is no tomorrow for us to be peaceful in. We have to be orderly on the instant.

When there is real danger time disappears, doesn't it? There is immediate action. But we do not see the danger of many of our problems and therefore we invent time as a means of overcoming them. Time

我忍不住要再讲一遍这个故事：一位优秀的门徒去拜访上帝，请求他传授真理，这个可怜的上帝说，"我的朋友，今天可真热啊，请给我杯水喝吧"。门徒于是出去敲最近一家的门，开门的是位年轻漂亮的姑娘，门徒爱上了她，然后他们结了婚，还生了几个孩子。后来有一天突然豪雨如注，下个不停，乃至洪水泛滥，街道被淹，房屋也被冲跑了。门徒抓紧妻子，肩背孩子，马上也要被洪水卷走了，这时他大叫："上帝啊，救救我吧！"这时上帝说："我要的那杯水呢？"

这是个很好的故事，因为我们大多数人都从时间的角度来思考。人依据时间而活。臆造出一个"未来"，一直是人们最热衷的逃避游戏。

我们以为假以时日我们自身便能有所改变，我们内心的秩序可以一点点建立、一日日增强。但时间并不会带来秩序或是和平，因此我们必须停止以渐进的方式思考。这就意味着我们可以安然栖身的明天并不存在，我们必须在当下这一刻即秩序井然。

若真正的危难当头，时间便消失了，不是吗？此时就会有刻不容缓的行动。但我们没有发现我们诸多问题的危险性，因而发明了时间作为克服它们的手段。时间是个骗子，因为它对于改变我们自己毫无

is a deceiver as it doesn't do a thing to help us bring about a change in ourselves. Time is a movement which man has divided into past, present and future, and as long as he divides it he will always be in conflict.

Is learning a matter of time? We have not learnt after all these thousands of years that there is a better way to live than by hating and killing each other. The problem of time is a very important one to understand if we are to resolve this life which we have helped to make as monstrous and meaningless as it is.

The first thing to understand is that we can look at time only with that freshness and innocency of mind which we have already been into. We are confused about our many problems and lost in that confusion. Now if one is lost in a wood, what is the first thing one does? One stops, doesn't one? One stops and looks round. But the more we are confused and lost in life the more we chase around, searching, asking, demanding, begging. So the first thing, if I may suggest it, is that you completely stop inwardly. And when you do stop inwardly, psychologically, your mind becomes very peaceful, very clear. Then you can really look at this question of time.

Problems exist only in time, that is when we meet an issue incompletely. This incomplete coming together with the issue creates the problem. When we meet a challenge partially, fragmentarily, or try to escape from it—that is, when we meet it without complete attention—we bring about a problem. And the problem continues so long as we continue to give it incomplete attention, so long as we hope to solve it one of these days.

Do you know what time is? Not by the watch, not chronological time, but psychological time? It is the interval between idea and action. An idea is for self-protection obviously; it is the idea of being secure. Action is always immediate; it is not of the past or of the future; to act must always be in

助益。时间是一场被人为割裂成过去、现在与未来的运动，只要人如此划分，他就将永远身陷冲突当中。

学习是一个时间问题吗？数千年来，我们从未学会一种更好的生活方式，我们依然相互憎恨、相互残杀。我们推波助澜，把生活变得如此可怕、如此没有意义，而若要解决生活这个问题，时间便是我们需要了解的一个重大课题。

我们首先要明白，唯有凭借之前所说的那颗清新纯真的心，我们方能看清时间的真相。我们对诸多问题感到困惑，并且迷失其中。然而，如果一个人在森林里迷了路，他要做的第一件事是什么？他会停下来，不是吗？他会停下来，查看四周。但我们越是困惑，越是迷失在生活中，就越是四处奔袭、追寻、盘问、索要、乞求。所以，请容我指出，首要的事便是让内心彻底停歇下来。当你内在、心理上的活动完全停歇下来，心就会变得格外安宁、格外清明，此时你才可以真正去审视时间这个问题。

问题仅存在于时间当中，也就是我们不完整地面对事情之时，是这种伴随事情而来的不完整造成了问题。当我们偏颇地、片段化地面对挑战，或者试图逃避它——也就是我们没有全神贯注地面对它时——问题便在所难免。只要我们继续心不在焉，只要我们寄希望于有朝一日能解决它，问题便会持续存在。

你可知道时间是什么？并非钟表的时间，也非日历上的时间，而是说心理时间是什么？它就是观念与行动之间的空隙。观念显然是为了自我保护而存在的，观念能带来安全感。而行动始终是当下的，它

the present, but action is so dangerous, so uncertain, that we conform to an idea which we hope will give us a certain safety.

Do look at this in yourself. You have an idea of what is right or wrong, or an ideological concept about yourself and society, and according to that idea you are going to act. Therefore the action is in conformity with that idea, approximating to the idea, and hence there is always conflict. There is the idea, the interval and action. And in that interval is the whole field of time. That interval is essentially thought. When you think you will be happy tomorrow, then you have an image of yourself achieving a certain result in time. Thought, through observation, through desire, and the continuity of that desire sustained by further thought, says, "Tomorrow I shall be happy. Tomorrow I shall have success. Tomorrow the world will be a beautiful place." So thought creates that interval which is time.

Now we are asking, can we put a stop to time? Can we live so completely that there is no tomorrow for thought to think about? Because time is sorrow. That is, yesterday or a thousand yesterday's ago, you loved, or you had a companion who has gone, and that memory remains and you are thinking about that pleasure and that pain—you are looking back, wishing, hoping, regretting, so thought, going over it again and again, breeds this thing we call sorrow and gives continuity to time.

So long as there is this interval of time which has been bred by thought, there must be sorrow, there must be continuity of fear. So one asks oneself can this interval come to an end? If you say, "Will it ever end?", then it is already an idea, something you want to achieve, and therefore you have an interval and you are caught again.

Now take the question of death which is an immense problem to most people. You know death, there it is walking every day by your side. Is

既不属于过去，也不属于未来，行动必定属于现在。但行动太危险、太不确定了，于是我们奉行某个观念，期待它能带来些许安全感。

请务必看看自己身上的这一点：你有是非对错的观念，或者对自己和社会抱有一些意识形态上的概念，然后按照那些观念去行动。所以行动是在迎合观念，在努力贴近观念，因而冲突连绵不断。观念、间隙、行动同时存在，那个间隙中有着时间的全部疆土，那个间隙实质上便是思想。当你以为自己明天会很快乐，你便塑造了一个经由时间取得某个结果的自我形象。借助见闻、借助欲望，以及另一些念头对欲望的延续、滋养，思想说："明天我就会快乐，明天我就会成功，明天世界将会变得美好。"因此是思想一手造成了时间这个间隙。

现在我们要问：我们能终止时间吗？我们能否如此全然地活在此刻，乃至根本没有什么明天可想？因为时间即是悲伤，也就是说，昨天或千万个昨日之前，你曾经爱过、拥有过的伴侣已然离去，那份记忆却留存了下来，你怀念那些快乐与痛楚，回望、渴盼、期许、懊悔交织在一起。所以思想一再反刍，便酿成了我们所谓悲伤，并且延续了时间。

思想催生的这个时间空隙只要存在，悲伤便在所难免，恐惧也必定得以延续。所以你问自己：这个间隙能否终止？如果你说："它究竟会终止吗？"那就已经是你想要达成的一个理念了，因而你已然有了空隙，并再次受困于其中。

现在我们以死亡为例，对大多数人来说，这是个巨大的问题。你

it possible to meet it so completely that you do not make a problem of it at all? In order to meet it in such a way all belief, all hope, all fear about it must come to an end, otherwise you are meeting this extraordinary thing with a conclusion, an image, with a premeditated anxiety, and therefore you are meeting it with time.

Time is the interval between the observer and the observed. That is, the observer, you, is afraid to meet this thing called death. You don't know what it means; you have all kinds of hopes and theories about it; you believe in reincarnation or resurrection, or in something called the soul, the atman, a spiritual entity which is timeless and which you call by different names. Now have you found out for yourself whether there is a soul? Or is it an idea that has been handed down to you? Is there something permanent, continuous, which is beyond thought? If thought can think about it, it is within the field of thought and therefore it cannot be permanent because there is nothing permanent within the field of thought. To discover that nothing is permanent is of tremendous importance for only then is the mind free, then you can look, and in that there is great joy.

You cannot be frightened of the unknown because you do not know what the unknown is and so there is nothing to be frightened of. Death is a word, and it is the word, the image, that creates fear. So can you look at death without the image of death? As long as the image exists from which springs thought, thought must always create fear. Then you either rationalize your fear of death and build a resistance against the inevitable or you invent innumerable beliefs to protect you from the fear of death. Hence there is a gap between you and the thing of which you are afraid. In this time-space interval there must be conflict which is fear, anxiety and self-pity. Thought, which breeds the fear of death, says, "Let's postpone it,

知道死亡，它每天都与你相伴而行。有没有可能如此全然地面对它，于是你根本不会把它变成问题？若要这样面对它，对它的所有信仰、所有希望、所有恐惧必须统统终止，否则你便是带着结论、形象以及预设的焦虑，来面对这件非凡的事物，因而是用时间在面对它。

时间是观察者与被观察者之间的隔阂。也就是说，你，这个观察者，害怕面对这件被称为"死亡"的事。你不知道它意味着什么，你对它抱有各式各样的期盼和理论，你相信轮回转世或者复活，或是所谓"灵魂""阿特曼"，一种永恒的精神实体，你给了它各种称呼。然而，你可曾亲自探索过灵魂究竟是否存在？抑或，那只是传承给你的一个概念罢了？究竟是否存在某种永恒的、持久的、超越思想的事物？倘若思想能思考它，那它就依然在思想的范畴之内，因此不可能是永恒的，因为思想的领域当中根本没有永恒可言。发现没什么是永恒的，这一点至关重要，因为只有此时心才是自由的，此时你才能去看，而这其中就有着无尽的喜悦。

你不可能害怕未知，因为你不知道未知是什么，所以没什么好怕的。死亡只是一个词，可正是这个词、这个意象造成了恐惧。因此，你能否看着死亡，却不怀有对死亡的意象？只要那个会引发思想的意象存在，思想就必定会造成恐惧。然后，你要么将你对死亡的恐惧合理化，竖起防御抵抗这件无可避免的事，要么发明出不计其数的信仰，来保护自己免于对死亡的恐惧。因此，你与你所惧怕的事物之间便产生了隔阂。在这个时空间隙当中，冲突，也就是恐惧、焦虑和自怜，便在所难免。思想催生了对死亡的恐惧，说，"让我们来推迟

let's avoid it, keep it as far away as possible, let's not think about it"—but you are thinking about it. When you say, "I won't think about it", you have already thought out how to avoid it. You are frightened of death because you have postponed it.

We have separated living from dying, and the interval between the living and the dying is fear. That interval, that time, is created by fear. Living is our daily torture, daily insult, sorrow and confusion, with occasional opening of a window over enchanted seas. That is what we call living, and we are afraid to die, which is to end this misery. We would rather cling to the known than face the unknown—the known being our house, our furniture, our family, our character, our work, our knowledge, our fame, our loneliness, our gods - that little thing that moves around incessantly within itself with its own limited pattern of embittered existence.

We think that living is always in the present and that dying is something that awaits us at a distant time. But we have never questioned whether this battle of everyday life is living at all. We want to know the truth about reincarnation, we want proof of the survival of the soul, we listen to the assertion of clairvoyants and to the conclusions of psychical research, but we never ask, never, how to live - to live with delight, with enchantment, with beauty every day. We have accepted life as it is with all its agony and despair and have got used to it, and think of death as something to be carefully avoided. But death is extraordinarily like life when we know how to live. You cannot live without dying. You cannot live if you do not die psychologically every minute. This is not an intellectual paradox. To live completely, wholly, every day as if it were a new loveliness, there must be dying to everything of yesterday, otherwise you live mechanically, and a mechanical mind can never know what love is or what freedom is.

它、避开它，离它越远越好，我们不要去想它"，可你就在想着它。当你说，"我不会去想它的"，你实际上已经在思考该如何避开它了。你畏惧死亡，正是因为你推迟了它。

我们把生与死分开了，而生死之间的空隙便是恐惧。那空隙，那时间，由恐惧所造。生活即是我们日复一日的折磨、侮辱、悲伤与困惑，偶尔能开窗一瞥令人那心醉神迷的海洋。这就是我们所谓"生活"，而我们却害怕死亡，害怕终结这场苦难。我们宁愿死守已知，也不愿面对未知，而已知就是我们的房子、家具、家庭、性格、工作、知识、名声、孤独以及各路神明——那个微不足道的东西自己不停地原地打转，固守着自身苦涩而有限的生存模式。

我们以为生活永远属于现在，而死亡则在遥远的未来等候着我们。我们从未质疑日常生活中的这场战斗究竟算不算生活。我们希望知道关于轮回的真相，我们想要证明灵魂在死后依然健在，我们听信通灵大师的断言，以及异能研究的结论，但我们从不探问如何生活——如何每天都活出愉悦、狂喜与美。我们接受了眼下的生活，以及它所有的痛苦和绝望，已经对它习以为常，同时又认为死亡是一件应当小心翼翼避免的事。然而，如果我们懂得了如何生活，死亡就会像生命一样不可思议。若不死去，你便无法真正去生活。如果不从心理上时刻死去，你就无法真正地活着。这并非一个思想上的悖论。若要每一天都全然地、完整地生活，就好像那是崭新而美妙的一天，就必须对昨日的一切死去，否则你就只会机械地过活，而一颗机械的心绝不可能懂得何为爱、何为自由。

Most of us are frightened of dying because we don't know what it means to live. We don't know how to live, therefore we don't know how to die. As long as we are frightened of life we shall be frightened of death. The man who is not frightened of life is not frightened of being completely insecure for he understands that inwardly, psychologically, there is no security. When there is no security there is an endless movement and then life and death are the same. The man who lives without conflict, who lives with beauty and love, is not frightened of death because to love is to die.

If you die to everything you know, including your family, your memory, everything you have felt, then death is a purification, a rejuvenating process; then death brings innocence and it is only the innocent who are passionate, not the people who believe or who want to find out what happens after death.

To find out actually what takes place when you die you must die. This isn't a joke. You must die—not physically but psychologically, inwardly, die to the things you have cherished and to the things you are bitter about. If you have died to one of your pleasures, the smallest or the greatest, naturally, without any enforcement or argument, then you will know what it means to die. To die is to have a mind that is completely empty of itself, empty of its daily longing, pleasure, and agonies. Death is a renewal, a mutation, in which thought does not function at all because thought is old. When there is death there is something totally new. Freedom from the known is death, and then you are living.

我们大多数人都畏惧死亡，因为我们不懂得生活意味着什么。我们不知道如何生活，因此也不知道如何去死。只要我们畏惧生活，我们便会畏惧死亡。不畏惧生活的人，便不会害怕彻底的不安全，因为他懂得，内在、心理上根本不存在所谓安全。当你不再追求安全感，就有了一种永无止境的运动，此时生死即为一体。一个人若是活得没有冲突，活出了美与爱，他是不会畏惧死亡的，因为爱即是死亡。

如果你对已知的一切死去，包括你的家庭、你的记忆、你感受到的一切，那么死亡便是一种净化，一个新生的过程，它会赋予你纯真。只有纯真者才能激情四溢，而不是那些抱持信仰的人，或者希望知道死后会如何的人。

若要发现死时究竟会发生什么，你就必须死去。这可不是一个玩笑。你必须死去——不是身体上死去，而是从心理上、从内在，对你珍视以及怨恨的一切死去。如果你对自己某件或大或小的快事死去，自然而然，毫不勉强，毫无争辩，那么你就会懂得死亡意味着什么。死亡意味着拥有一颗彻底清空了自己、清空了日常的渴望、欢愉和痛苦的心。死亡是一种新生、一种突变，其中没有任何思想活动，因为思想是陈旧的。有了死亡，就有了某种全新的东西。从已知中解脱便是死亡，此时你方能真正地生活。

PART 10
第十部分

Love

爱

Tge demand to be safe in relationship inevitably breeds sorrow and fear. This seeking for security is inviting insecurity. Have you ever found security in any of your relationships? Have you? Most of us want the security of loving and being loved, but is there love when each one of us is seeking his own security, his own particular path? We are not loved because we don't know how to love.

What is love? The word is so loaded and corrupted that I hardly like to use it. Everybody talks of love—every magazine and newspaper and every missionary talks everlastingly of love. I love my country, I love my king, I love some book, I love that mountain, I love pleasure, I love my wife, I love God. Is love an idea? If it is, it can be cultivated, nourished, cherished, pushed around, twisted in any way you like. When you say you love God what does it mean? It means that you love a projection of your own imagination, a projection of yourself clothed in certain forms of respectability according to what you think is noble and holy; so to say, "I love God", is absolute nonsense. When you worship God you are worshipping yourself—and that is not love.

Because we cannot solve this human thing called love we run away into abstractions. Love may be the ultimate solution to all man's difficulties, problems and travails, so how are we going to find out what love is? By merely defining it? The church has defined it one way, society another and there are all sorts of deviations and perversions. Adoring someone, sleeping

　　只要在关系中求取安全感，便必定会招来悲伤与恐惧。对安全感的这份追求，便是在邀约不安全。你可曾在任何关系中找到过安全？有吗？我们大多数人都希望得到爱与被爱的安全感，但是，当我们每个人都在追求自身的安全感、自己特定的轨迹，爱还会存在吗？我们没有被爱，是因为我们不懂得如何去爱。

　　爱是什么？这个词已经变得如此沉重、如此败坏，我几乎不愿再使用它。每个人都谈论爱——每本杂志、每家报纸、每个教士都没完没了地谈论着爱。我爱我的国家，我爱我的国王，我爱某本书，我爱那座山，我爱享乐，我爱我的妻子，我爱上帝。爱是一个概念吗？如果是，那么它就可以被培育、被滋养、被珍视、被摆布，被随心所欲地扭曲。当你说你爱上帝，那是什么意思？那意味着，你爱的是你自身想象的一种化身，是你按照自己对高尚、神圣的想法，投射出了一个罩以体面外衣的自己。所以，说"我爱上帝"，是彻头彻尾的无稽之谈。当你膜拜上帝，你就是在膜拜自己，而这不是爱。

　　由于无法解决人类所谓"爱"这个问题，我们便遁入抽象的概念。爱或许便是人类所有的困境、难题和痛苦的终极解答，那么我们要如何厘清爱是什么呢？仅仅给它下个定义就够了吗？教堂给它一个定义，社会给它另一个定义，各式各样的偏差和扭曲层出不穷。爱慕

with someone, the emotional exchange, the companionship—is that what we mean by love? That has been the norm, the pattern, and it has become so tremendously personal, sensuous, and limited that religions have declared that love is something much more than this. In what they call human love they see there is pleasure, competition, jealousy, the desire to possess, to hold, to control and to interfere with another's thinking, and knowing the complexity of all this they say there must be another kind of love, divine, beautiful, untouched, uncorrupted.

Throughout the world, so-called holy men have maintained that to look at a woman is something totally wrong: they say you cannot come near to God if you indulge in sex, therefore they push it aside although they are eaten up with it. But by denying sexuality they put out their eyes and cut out their tongues for they deny the whole beauty of the earth. They have starved their hearts and minds; they are dehydrated human beings; they have banished beauty because beauty is associated with woman.

Can love be divided into the sacred and the profane, the human and the divine, or is there only love? Is love of the one and not of the many? If I say, "I love you", does that exclude the love of the other? Is love personal or impersonal? Moral or immoral? Family or non-family? If you love mankind can you love the particular? Is love sentiment? Is love emotion? Is love pleasure and desire? All these questions indicate, don't they, that we have ideas about love, ideas about what it should or should not be, a pattern or a code developed by the culture in which we live.

So to go into the question of what love is we must first free it from the encrustation of centuries, put away all ideals and ideologies of what it should or should not be. To divide anything into what should be and what is, is the most deceptive way of dealing with life.

某人、同床共枕、情感交流、互相陪伴——这就是我们所说的爱吗？那些已经成了规范和模式，爱也变得极其个人化，变得非常局限，并且注重感官享受，于是各派宗教都声称，爱远远超越了这一切。在他们所谓"凡人之爱"当中，他们发现存在着快感、竞争、嫉妒，存在着占有、执着、控制以及干涉他人想法的欲望。知道了这一切的复杂性，他们于是说必须得有另一种爱，神圣、美丽、未被腐蚀、纯洁无瑕。

全世界所谓"圣人"都坚称，看女人是大错特错的事。他们说，倘若你耽于性事，便无法接近上帝，因此他们戒除了性，尽管内心备受煎熬。但是，戒除性欲使他们就像挖掉了双眼、割断了舌头，因为他们拒绝了大地之美。他们让自己的心灵和头脑饥渴无比，他们成了干涸的人类。他们摒弃了美，因为美与女人紧密相关。

爱能被划分为神圣之爱与世俗之爱、凡人之爱与圣洁之爱吗？抑或存在的只有爱罢了？爱只属于个人而不属于众人吗？如果我说："我爱你"，那就排除了对其他人的爱吗？爱是个人的还是非个人的？是道德的还是不道德的？属于家庭还是不属于家庭？如果你爱全人类，你还会不会爱上某个人？爱是感触吗？爱是情绪吗？爱是快感和欲望吗？这些问题都说明，我们对爱抱有各种概念，关于它应当是什么或不应是什么的观点，以及我们所处的文化培植出来的模式或准则，不是吗？

因此，若要探究"爱是什么"这个问题，我们就必须首先摆脱数百年来的积淀，摒弃一切"爱应当如何"或"爱不应如何"的理想或

Now how am I going to find out what this flame is which we call love —not how to express it to another but what it means in itself? I will first reject what the church, what society, what my parents and friends, what every person and every book has said about it because I want to find out for myself what it is. Here is an enormous problem that involves the whole of mankind, there have been a thousand ways of defining it and I myself am caught in some pattern or other according to what I like or enjoy at the moment—so shouldn't I, in order to understand it, first free myself from my own inclinations and prejudices? I am confused, torn by my own desires, so I say to myself, "First clear up your own confusion. Perhaps you may be able to discover what love is through what it is not."

The government says, "Go and kill for the love of your country". Is that love? Religion says, "Give up sex for the love of God". Is that love? Is love desire? Don't say no. For most of us it is—desire with pleasure, the pleasure that is derived through the senses, through sexual attachment and fulfilment. I am not against sex, but see what is involved in it. What sex gives you momentarily is the total abandonment of yourself, then you are back again with your turmoil, so you want a repetition over and over again of that state in which there is no worry, no problem, no self.

You say you love your wife. In that love is involved sexual pleasure, the pleasure of having someone in the house to look after your children, to cook. You depend on her; she has given you her body, her emotions, her encouragement, a certain feeling of security and well-being. Then she turns away from you; she gets bored or goes off with someone else, and your whole emotional balance is destroyed, and this disturbance, which you don't like, is called jealousy. There is pain in it, anxiety, hate and violence. So what you are really saying is, "As long as you belong to me I love you but

者概念。把任何事物划分为"应当如何"与"现在如何"，都是最自欺欺人的生活态度。

那么我要如何才能找到我们称为"爱"的这簇火焰？并非如何向别人表达爱，而是爱本身的含义是什么？首先，我会抛开教堂、社会、我的父母和朋友以及所有人、所有书本对爱的说法，因为我想亲自探明爱是什么。这是一个牵扯到全人类的庞大问题，对它已经有了上千种定义，我自己也因为一时的喜好而困在了某个模式当中。因此，为了了解它，我难道不应该首先把自己从各种倾向与偏见当中解放出来吗？我相当困惑，被自己的各种欲望撕扯，所以我对自己说："先厘清你自己的困惑，也许你就能通过了解爱不是什么来发现爱是什么了。"

政府说："为了国家，你要上阵杀敌。"那是爱吗？宗教则说："为了爱上帝，你得断除性事。"那是爱吗？爱是欲望吗？不要说不是。对我们大多数人而言，爱就是欲望——伴随着快感的欲望，快感则通过感官享受、通过性依恋及性满足而来。我并不反对性事，只是要看清其中隐含着什么。性可以让你在片刻间彻底摒弃自我，但随后你又回到了自己的混乱当中。所以你渴望一次次地重温那种状态，那种没有忧虑、没有问题的忘我境界。

你说你爱你的妻子，那份爱当中就包含了性快感，以及家里有个人照看孩子、煮饭带来的快乐。你依赖她，她给了你她的身体、她的感情、她的鼓励，给了你一种安全感和幸福感。可她后来离你而去了，她厌倦了，或者跟别人私奔了，于是你情感上的整个平衡就被打

the moment you don't I begin to hate you. As long as I can rely on you to satisfy my demands, sexual and otherwise, I love you, but the moment you cease to supply what I want I don't like you."

So there is antagonism between you, there is separation, and when you feel separate from another there is no love. But if you can live with your wife without thought creating all these contradictory states, these endless quarrels in yourself, then perhaps—perhaps—you will know what love is. Then you are completely free and so is she, whereas if you depend on her for all your pleasure you are a slave to her. So when one loves there must be freedom, not only from the other person but from oneself.

This belonging to another, being psychologically nourished by another, depending on another—in all this there must always be anxiety, fear, jealousy, guilt, and so long as there is fear there is no love; a mind ridden with sorrow will never know what love is; sentimentality and emotionalism have nothing whatsoever to do with love. And so love is not to do with pleasure and desire.

Love is not the product of thought which is the past. Thought cannot possibly cultivate love. Love is not hedged about and caught in jealousy, for jealousy is of the past. Love is always active present. It is not "I will love" or "I have loved". If you know love you will not follow anybody. Love does not obey. When you love there is neither respect nor disrespect.

Don't you know what it means really to love somebody—to love without hate, without jealousy, without anger, without wanting to interfere with what he is doing or thinking, without condemning, without comparing —don't you know what it means? Where there is love is there comparison? When you love someone with all your heart, with all your mind, with all your body, with your entire being, is there comparison? When you totally

破了。你不喜欢这种打扰，这就是所谓"嫉妒"，其中还有痛苦、焦虑、憎恨和暴力。因此，实际上你的潜台词是："只要你属于我，我就爱你，可一旦你不再属于我，我就开始恨你。只要我能依靠你来满足我的欲望，无论是性欲还是别的，我就爱你。然而一旦你停止供给我所需的，我就不喜欢你了。"

因此你们之间存在一种敌对、一种分裂，而当你感觉到彼此是分离的，爱就不在了。但是，如果你能与你的妻子生活在一起，却没有思想在你内心制造的所有对立状态和无尽的争吵，那么也许——只是也许——你就能知道爱是什么了。然后你就彻底自由了，她也一样。然而，一旦你依赖她获取快感，你就成了她的奴隶。所以，若要去爱，就必须拥有自由，不仅仅是从对方那里，也包括从自身当中解脱出来的自由。

这份对他人的归属感、依赖感，精神上依靠他人来滋养的状态，必定包含着焦虑、恐惧、嫉妒、负疚，而只要有恐惧，就不可能有爱。一颗被哀伤折磨的心，永远无法懂得爱是什么。多愁善感跟感情用事都与爱没有丝毫干系。因此，爱与快感和欲望毫不相干。

爱并非思想即过去的产物，思想绝不可能培育出爱。爱不会被嫉妒所围困，因为嫉妒属于过去，而爱永远属于鲜活的现在。它不是"我将去爱"或者"我爱过了"。如果你懂得了爱，你便不会追随任何人。爱不会臣服，当你爱着，便无所谓尊敬或是不敬。

你不知道真正爱一个人是什么意思吗？去爱，没有怨恨，没有嫉妒，没有愤怒，不想干涉他的做法或者想法，不加谴责，不做比

abandon yourself to that love there is not the other.

Does love have responsibility and duty, and will it use those words? When you do something out of duty is there any love in it? In duty there is no love. The structure of duty in which the human being is caught is destroying him. So long as you are compelled to do something because it is your duty you don't love what you are doing. When there is love there is no duty and no responsibility.

Most parents unfortunately think they are responsible for their children and their sense of responsibility takes the form of telling them what they should do and what they should not do, what they should become and what they should not become. The parents want their children to have a secure position in society. What they call responsibility is part of that respectability they worship; and it seems to me that where there is respectability there is no order; they are concerned only with becoming a perfect bourgeois. When they prepare their children to fit into society they are perpetuating war, conflict and brutality. Do you call that care and love?

Really to care is to care as you would for a tree or a plant, watering it, studying its needs, the best soil for it, looking after it with gentleness and tenderness—but when you prepare your children to fit into society you are preparing them to be killed. If you loved your children you would have no war.

When you lose someone you love you shed tears—are your tears for yourself or for the one who is dead? Are you crying for yourself or for another? Have you ever cried for another? Have you ever cried for your son who was killed on the battlefield? You have cried, but do those tears come out of self-pity or have you cried because a human being has been killed? If you cry out of self-pity your tears have no meaning because you

较——你不知道那意味着什么吗？有爱的地方还会有比较吗？当你用你的一整颗心，用你的全部头脑、全部身体，用你的整个生命去爱一个人，你还会比较吗？当你为爱彻底舍弃了自己，比较根本没有容身之地。

爱里有责任和义务吗？爱会用到那些字眼吗？当你出于义务做什么的时候，其中还有爱吗？义务当中没有爱。围困人类的义务枷锁正在毁掉人类。只要你被迫做什么，因为那是你的义务，你便不爱你所做的事。有了爱，便没有责任和义务可言。

不幸的是，大多数父母都自认为对孩子负有责任，而他们的责任感表现为告诉孩子该做什么，不该做什么，该成为什么，不该成为什么。父母希望自己的孩子在社会上拥有牢靠的职位。他们所谓责任，是他们所崇拜的体面生活的一部分。而在我看来，追求体面就没有秩序可言，他们所关心的只是成为一名地道的中产阶级。当他们培养自己的孩子适应社会，他们便是在无止境地延续战争、冲突与暴行。你就把那些称为关怀和爱吗？

真正的关怀就像照料一棵树或是一株植物，你灌溉它，研究它的需要，为它提供最好的土壤，细心、温柔地照顾它。然而，当你培养你的孩子去适应社会，你便在准备让他们日后惨遭屠戮。如果你爱你的孩子，你就不会发动战争。

当失去了所爱的人，你会流泪，可你的眼泪是为自己而流，还是为逝者而流？你是为自己还是为别人哭泣？你可曾为你战死沙场的儿子哭泣？你哭过，但那些眼泪是出于自怜，还是因为一个生命被杀害

are concerned about yourself. If you are crying because you are bereft of one in whom you have invested a great deal of affection, it was not really affection. When you cry for your brother who dies cry for him. It is very easy to cry for yourself because he is gone. Apparently you are crying because your heart is touched, but it is not touched for him, it is only touched by self-pity and self-pity makes you hard, encloses you, makes you dull and stupid.

When you cry for yourself, is it love—crying because you are lonely, because you have been left, because you are no longer powerful—complaining of your lot, your environment—always you in tears? If you understand this, which means to come in contact with it as directly as you would touch a tree or a pillar or a hand, then you will see that sorrow is self-created, sorrow is created by thought, sorrow is the outcome of time. I had my brother three years ago, now he is dead, now I am lonely, aching, there is no one to whom I can look for comfort or companionship, and it brings tears to my eyes.

You can see all this happening inside yourself if you watch it. You can see it fully, completely, in one glance, not take analytical time over it. You can see in a moment the whole structure and nature of this shoddy little thing called "me", my tears, my family, my nation, my belief, my religion —all that ugliness, it is all inside you. When you see it with your heart, not with your mind, when you see it from the very bottom of your heart, then you have the key that will end sorrow.

Sorrow and love cannot go together, but in the Christian world they have idealized suffering, put it on a cross and worshipped it, implying that you can never escape from suffering except through that one particular door, and this is the whole structure of an exploiting religious society.

了？如果你哭泣是出于自怜，你的眼泪便没有意义，因为你关心的是你自己。如果你哭泣，是因为你失去一个在他身上投入了大量关爱的人，那就不是真正的关爱。当你为逝去的兄弟哭泣，那就只为他而流泪。你很容易因为他不在了而为自己流泪。你哭泣，显然是因为你内心受到了触动，但并非为他所触动，你只是因为自怜才感伤，而自怜让你变得冷漠、封闭、麻木以及愚蠢。

当你为自己而哭泣，那是爱吗？你哭泣，是因为你孤独，因为你被抛弃了，因为你不再呼风唤雨——抱怨你的命运、你的境遇——总是"你"在哭泣，那是爱吗？如果你懂得了这一点，直接领会到这一点，就像你碰触一棵树、一根柱子或是一只手那样直接，你便会发现悲伤由自我所造，由思想所造，悲伤即是时间的产物。三年前我的兄弟还健在，现在他去世了，我孤单、痛苦，再也没人给我慰藉和陪伴，这让我泪盈于睫。

只要你观察，就可以看到这些都在你内心发生着。你一瞥即可充分、彻底地看清这一点，根本无须花费时间去分析它。你瞬间即可看清所谓"我"，这个卑劣狭隘的东西的整个结构和本质，我的眼泪，我的家庭，我的国家，我的信仰，我的宗教——所有的丑陋，都藏在你内心里面。当你用心而不是用头脑看到了这一点，当你从心底的最深处看清了这一点，你便掌握了终止悲伤的钥匙。

悲伤与爱无法同行，但在基督教的世界中，他们把痛苦理想化了，把它放在了十字架上顶礼膜拜，寓意你永远无法逃脱痛苦，除非穿过他们那扇独特的门，而这正体现宗教社团剥削世人的整个架构。

So when you ask what love is, you may be too frightened to see the answer. It may mean complete upheaval; it may break up the family; you may discover that you do not love your wife or husband or children—do you? —you may have to shatter the house you have built, you may never go back to the temple.

But if you still want to find out, you will see that fear is not love, dependence is not love, jealousy is not love, possessiveness and domination are not love, responsibility and duty are not love, self-pity is not love, the agony of not being loved is not love, love is not the opposite of hate any more than humility is the opposite of vanity. So if you can eliminate all these, not by forcing them but by washing them away as the rain washes the dust of many days from a leaf, then perhaps you will come upon this strange flower which man always hungers after.

If you have not got love—not just in little drops but in abundance —if you are not filled with it—the world will go to disaster. You know intellectually that the unity of mankind is essential and that love is the only way, but who is going to teach you how to love? Will any authority, any method, any system, tell you how to love? If anyone tells you, it is not love. Can you say, "I will practise love. I will sit down day after day and think about it. I will practise being kind and gentle and force myself to pay attention to others"? Do you mean to say that you can discipline yourself to love, exercise the will to love? When you exercise discipline and will to love, love goes out of the window. By practising some method or system of loving you may become extraordinarily clever or more kindly or get into a state of non-violence, but that has nothing whatsoever to do with love.

In this torn desert world there is no love because pleasure and desire play the greatest roles, yet without love your daily life has no meaning. And

因此，当你问爱是什么，你也许会太过恐惧，不敢去看答案。爱也许意味着彻底的颠覆，它可能会拆散家庭，你或许会发现你根本不爱你的妻子、丈夫或是孩子——你真的爱他们吗？——你也许不得不毁掉自己亲手搭建的家园，你可能再也不会造访寺庙。

然而，如果你仍想探明真相，你便会发现恐惧不是爱，依赖不是爱，嫉妒不是爱，占有控制不是爱，责任义务不是爱，自怨自艾不是爱，不被人爱的痛苦不是爱，爱不是恨的反面，正如谦卑不是自负的反面。因此，如果你能消除这一切，不加勉强，而是就像雨水洗净树叶上多日来的尘土一般，将它们涤荡一清，那么你或许便会邂逅人类长久以来所渴望的那朵奇葩。

倘若你尚未拥有爱——不是细微点滴，而是丰盈的爱——如果你内心没有充满爱，这个世界将在劫难逃。道理上你明白，全人类团结起来至关重要，爱是唯一的出路，但谁能教你如何去爱呢？有任何一种权威、方法、体系能告诉你如何去爱吗？如果有人这么做，那就不是爱。"我会练习爱，我会日复一日坐下来思考爱，我会练习友善与温柔，命令自己去关心他人"，你能这么说吗？你的意思是不是，你可以训练自己去爱，运用意志力去爱？当你运用训练和意志力去爱，爱就溜出了窗外。通过练习某些爱的方法或者体系，你也许会变得异常聪明或者更加友善，或是进入一种非暴力状态，但那与爱没有半点关系。

这个荒芜破碎的世界上没有爱，因为快感和欲望主宰了一切，然而没有爱，你每日的生活便失去了意义。而如果没有美，你便无法拥

you cannot have love if there is no beauty. Beauty is not something you see —not a beautiful tree, a beautiful picture, a beautiful building or a beautiful woman. There is beauty only when your heart and mind know what love is. Without love and that sense of beauty there is no virtue, and you know very well that, do what you will, improve society, feed the poor, you will only be creating more mischief, for without love there is only ugliness and poverty in your own heart and mind. But when there is love and beauty, whatever you do is right, whatever you do is in order. If you know how to love, then you can do what you like because it will solve all other problems.

So we reach the point: can the mind come upon love without discipline, without thought, without enforcement, without any book, any teacher or leader—come upon it as one comes upon a lovely sunset?

It seems to me that one thing is absolutely necessary and that is passion without motive—passion that is not the result of some commitment or attachment, passion that is not lust. A man who does not know what passion is will never know love because love can come into being only when there is total self-abandonment.

A mind that is seeking is not a passionate mind and to come upon love without seeking it is the only way to find it—to come upon it unknowingly and not as the result of any effort or experience. Such a love, you will find, is not of time; such a love is both personal and impersonal, is both the one and the many. Like a flower that has perfume you can smell it or pass it by. That flower is for everybody and for the one who takes trouble to breathe it deeply and look at it with delight. Whether one is very near in the garden, or very far away, it is the same to the flower because it is full of that perfume and therefore it is sharing with everybody.

Love is something that is new, fresh, alive. It has no yesterday and no

有爱。美并非你肉眼所见的东西———棵美丽的树，一幅漂亮的画，一栋精美的建筑，或是一个漂亮的女人。只有当你的内心与头脑都懂得了爱为何物，美才会出现。没有爱与那样的美，亦无美德可言。你非常清楚，无论你做什么——改良社会，救济穷人——都只会引发更多的不幸，因为没有爱，你的头脑和内心就只有丑陋和贫穷。然而，一旦有了爱与美，无论你做什么都是正确的，都将秩序井然。只要你懂得了如何去爱，你即可随心所欲地行动，因为爱将会解决所有的问题。

所以我们触及了核心问题：心能不能邂逅爱，而无须修炼、无须思虑、无须强制，也无须任何书本、任何导师或是任何领袖，就像偶遇一场美丽的日落一样与爱邂逅？

在我看来，有一件事是绝对必要的，那便是没有动机的热情——那股激情并非某种承诺或执着的产物，也绝非肉欲。一个不知道激情为何物的人，永远不会懂得爱，因为只有彻底舍弃了自我，爱才会到来。

一颗还在追寻的心便不是一颗激情四溢的心，不加追寻地邂逅爱，是找到它的唯一方式——毫不知情地与它邂逅，而非任何努力或是经验的结果。你会发现，这样的一种爱，与时间无关，它既个人化，又与个人无关，它兼顾个体以及众人。就像一朵芬芳四溢的花，你可以嗅它的香气，也可从旁经过。那朵花为所有人绽放，也为那个肯深深呼吸并开心凝视的人绽放。无论那个人近在花园还是远在天边，对那朵花来说并无不同，因为它花香四溢，所以能与天下人一起分享。

爱是新鲜、清新、生机勃勃的事物，既没有昨日，也没有明天，

tomorrow. It is beyond the turmoil of thought. It is only the innocent mind which knows what love is, and the innocent mind can live in the world which is not innocent. To find this extraordinary thing which man has sought endlessly through sacrifice, through worship, through relationship, through sex, through every form of pleasure and pain, is only possible when thought comes to understand itself and comes naturally to an end. Then love has no opposite, then love has no conflict.

You may ask, "If I find such a love, what happens to my wife, my children, my family? They must have security." When you put such a question you have never been outside the field of thought, the field of consciousness. When once you have been outside that field you will never ask such a question because then you will know what love is in which there is no thought and therefore no time. You may read this mesmerized and enchanted, but actually to go beyond thought and time—which means going beyond sorrow—is to be aware that there is a different dimension called love.

But you don't know how to come to this extraordinary fount—so what do you do? If you don't know what to do, you do nothing, don't you? Absolutely nothing. Then inwardly you are completely silent. Do you understand what that means? It means that you are not seeking, not wanting, not pursuing; there is no centre at all. Then there is love.

它超越了思想的混乱。只有纯真的心才懂得爱是什么，而纯真的心是可以生活在这个并不纯真的世界上的。人没完没了地通过牺牲、膜拜、关系、性以及各式各样的苦与乐，来寻找爱这样非凡的事物。只有当思想看清了自己，并自然而然地停歇下来，才有可能发现它。此时的爱没有对立面，也不存在冲突。

你也许会问："如果我找到了这样的爱，我的妻子、我的孩子、我的家庭会怎样？他们必须得到保障。"当你提出这样一个问题，就说明你从未走出思想的领地、意识的领地。一旦你走出了那些领域，你就绝不会提出这样的问题，因为那时你便会懂得爱是什么，那样的爱里没有思想，因而时间也消失了。你也许读了这些话之后感觉心醉神迷，但要真的超越思想和时间——亦即超越悲伤——就要了知还有另一个被称为"爱"的维度。

但你不知道如何找到这股不可思议的源泉——那你会怎么办？如果你不知道怎么办，你就会什么都不做，对吗？完完全全什么都不做，然后你的内心就彻底安静了下来。你知道这意味着什么吗？意味着你不再寻找、不再渴望、不再追求，中心已彻底不在，此时爱便出现了。

PART 11
第十一部分

To Look and to Listen—Art
—Beauty—Austerity—Images—
Problems—Space

看和听——艺术——美——简
朴——形象——问题——空间

We have been enquiring into the nature of love and have come to a point, I think, which needs much greater penetration, a much greater awareness of the issue. We have discovered that for most people love means comfort, security, a guarantee for the rest of their lives of continuous emotional satisfaction. Then someone like me comes along and says, "Is that really love?" and questions you and asks you to look inside yourself. And you try not to look because it is very disturbing—you would rather discuss the soul or the political or economic situation—but when you are driven into a corner to look, you realize that what you have always thought of as love is not love at all; it is a mutual gratification, a mutual exploitation.

When I say, "Love has no tomorrow and no yesterday", or, "When there is no centre then there is love", it has reality for me but not for you. You may quote it and make it into a formula but that has no validity. You have to see it for yourself, but to do so there must be freedom to look, freedom from all condemnation, all judgement all agreeing or disagreeing.

Now, to look is one of the most difficult things in life—or to listen— to look and listen are the same. If your eyes are blinded with your worries, you cannot see the beauty of the sunset. Most of us have lost touch with nature. Civilization is tending more and more towards large cities; we are becoming more and more an urban people, living in crowded apartments and having very little space even to look at the sky of an evening and

我们已经探讨了爱的本质，接下来的问题，我认为需要我们更为深入地洞悉和觉察。我们已经发现，对大多数人来说，爱意味着舒适、安全，一份余生都在情感上得到持续满足的保障。然后我这样的一个人过来说："那真的是爱吗？"他质疑你，然后请你审视自己的内心。可你想方设法不去看，因为那令你非常不安，你宁愿讨论灵魂，或者政治、经济局势。但是，当你被逼到角落，不得不去看时，你便会发现，你一直所认为的爱根本就不是爱，而只不过是一种相互满足、相互剥削罢了。

当我说："爱既没有明天，也没有昨日"，或者"当中心消失，爱才会出现"，这对我来说是真实的，对你却不是。你可以引用这些句子，把它变成公式，但那毫无意义。你得亲自看清楚，但要做到这一点，你就必须有看的自由，必须从所有的谴责、所有的评判、所有的赞同或是反对当中解脱出来。

然而，"看"或者聆听——看和听是一回事——是生命中最为艰难的事之一。如果你的双眼因忧虑而盲目，你便看不到落日的美。我们大多数人都失去了与自然的联系。文明越来越趋近大城市，我们也变得越来越像一个都市人，住在拥挤的公寓里，甚至都没有空间去看看日暮与清晨的天空，因而与许许多多的美都断了联系。我不知道你

morning, and therefore we are losing touch with a great deal of beauty. I don't know if you have noticed how few of us look at a sunrise or a sunset or the moonlight or the reflection of light on water.

Having lost touch with nature we naturally tend to develop intellectual capacities. We read a great many books, go to a great many museums and concerts, watch television and have many other entertainments. We quote endlessly from other people's ideas and think and talk a great deal about art. Why is it that we depend so much upon art? Is it a form of escape, of stimulation? If you are directly in contact with nature; if you watch the movement of a bird on the wing, see the beauty of every movement of the sky, watch the shadows on the hills or the beauty on the face of another, do you think you will want to go to any museum to look at any picture? Perhaps it is because you do not know how to look at all the things about you that you resort to some form of drug to stimulate you to see better.

There is a story of a religious teacher who used to talk every morning to his disciples. One morning he got on to the platform and was just about to begin when a little bird came and sat on the window sill and began to sing, and sang away with full heart. Then it stopped and flew away and the teacher said, "The sermon for this morning is over".

It seems to me that one of our greatest difficulties is to see for ourselves really clearly, not only outward things but inward life. When we say we see a tree or a flower or a person, do we actually see them? Or do we merely see the image that the word has created? That is, when you look at a tree or at a cloud of an evening full of light and delight, do you actually see it, not only with your eyes and intellectually, but totally, completely?

Have you ever experimented with looking at an objective thing like a tree without any of the associations, any of the knowledge you have

是否注意到，我们极少有人去观赏日升日落，或者水面上的月色与粼粼波光。

　　失去了与自然的联系，我们便自然会更加注重发展头脑的能力。我们阅读大量的书籍，频繁光顾博物馆与音乐会，看电视，以及拥有其他各种娱乐形式。我们没完没了地引用他人的思想，对于艺术也是费心思索、高谈阔论。为什么我们如此依赖艺术？那是不是一种逃避、一种刺激？如果你与自然有直接的接触，如果你注视展翅飞翔的小鸟，观赏天空的变幻之美，凝望群山之上的投影，或是一张美丽的脸庞，你觉得你还会想去任何一家博物馆欣赏图画吗？或许正是因为你不知如何去看周围的万物，你才会求助于某种药物来刺激你看得更清楚。

　　有一个故事，讲的是一位宗教师父常常在早上给弟子们一番训导。一天早上，他走上讲台，正打算开始，此时一只小鸟飞过来落在窗台上，开始全心全意地唱起歌来。不久后它停止了歌唱，飞走了，这时师父说道："今早的训导结束了。"

　　在我看来，我们最大的难题之一，便是亲自看清真相，不仅看清外在的事物，也包括我们内在的生活。当我们说看到了一棵树、一朵花或是一个人，我们真的看到它们了吗？抑或，我们见到的只是词语编织的意象？也就是说，当你凝望一棵树，或是充满了光彩与欣喜的一抹晚霞，你是不是真的看到了它，不仅仅用你的眼睛和头脑，而是全然地、完整地见到了它？

　　你可曾试过看着一个客观事物，比如一棵树，不做任何联想，

acquired about it, without any prejudice, any judgement, any words forming a screen between you and the tree and preventing you from seeing it as it actually is? Try it and see what actually takes place when you observe the tree with all your being, with the totality of your energy. In that intensity you will find that there is no observer at all; there is only attention. It is when there is inattention that there is the observer and the observed. When you are looking at something with complete attention there is no space for a conception, a formula or a memory. This is important to understand because we are going into something which requires very careful investigation.

It is only a mind that looks at a tree or the stars or the sparkling waters of a river with complete self-abandonment that knows what beauty is, and when we are actually seeing we are in a state of love. We generally know beauty through comparison or through what man has put together, which means that we attribute beauty to some object. I see what I consider to be a beautiful building and that beauty I appreciate because of my knowledge of architecture and by comparing it with other buildings I have seen. But now I am asking myself, "Is there a beauty without object?" When there is an observer who is the censor, the experiencer, the thinker, there is no beauty because beauty is something external, something the observer looks at and judges, but when there is no observer—and this demands a great deal of meditation, of enquiry—then there is beauty without the object.

Beauty lies in the total abandonment of the observer and the observed and there can be self-abandonment only when there is total austerity— not the austerity of the priest with its harshness, its sanctions, rules and obedience—not austerity in clothes, ideas, food and behaviour—but the austerity of being totally simple which is complete humility. Then there is no achieving, no ladder to climb; there is only the first step and the first

不带有之前获得的相关知识，不让任何偏见、任何评判、任何言语构成你与那棵树之间的屏障，不让它们妨碍你如实地见到那棵树？试一试，看看当你用你的整个生命、用你的全部精力去观察那棵树时，究竟会发生什么。在那样的强度之下，你会发现观察者彻底不在了，只剩下那份全然的关注。只有漫不经心时观察者和所观之物才会出现。当你用全部的注意力去看，概念、公式或记忆就没有了存在的空间。理解这一点非常重要，因为我们所探讨的问题需要十分周密的考察。

当一颗心注视一棵树，凝望漫天繁星或是河面上的波光，只有它彻底摒弃了自我，方能懂得美是什么，只有当我们真正看清了，方能沉浸在爱当中。我们通常是借助比较或者人为的方式来了解美的，也就是说，我们认为美是某些客体具有的品质。我见到了我所认为的美丽建筑，我欣赏那种美，是因为我有建筑学知识，与我之前见过的其他建筑做了对比，才认为它很美。但现在我问自己："是否存在一种美是没有客体的？"当有了观察者，也就是审查者、经验者、思考者，就没有了美，因为那样美就成了外在的东西，成了观察者去看、去评判的东西。然而，当没有了观察者——而这需要深入的冥想与探究——此时没有客体的美便出现了。

美存在于对观察者与被观察者的彻底摒弃当中，而只有完全的简朴方能带来自我摒弃。那种简朴并非教士的苦行、惩戒、条规以及臣服，也非衣食、观念、行为的朴素，而是指完全简单，也就是完全谦卑的那样一种简朴。此时便不再有成就与攀登的阶梯，而只有最初那

step is the everlasting step.

Say you are walking by yourself or with somebody and you have stopped talking. You are surrounded by nature and there is no dog barking, no noise of a car passing or even the flutter of a bird. You are completely silent and nature around you is also wholly silent. In that state of silence both in the observer and the observed—when the observer is not translating what he observes into thought—in that silence there is a different quality of beauty. There is neither nature nor the observer. There is a state of mind wholly, completely, alone; it is alone—not in isolation —alone in stillness and that stillness is beauty. When you love, is there an observer? There is an observer only when love is desire and pleasure. When desire and pleasure are not associated with love, then love is intense. It is, like beauty, something totally new every day. As I have said, it has no today and no tomorrow.

It is only when we see without any preconception, any image, that we are able to be in direct contact with anything in life. All our relationships are really imaginary—that is, based on an image formed by thought. If I have an image about you and you have an image about me, naturally we don't see each other at all as we actually are. What we see is the images we have formed about each other which prevent us from being in contact, and that is why our relationships go wrong.

When I say I know you, I mean I knew you yesterday. I do not know you actually now. All I know is my image of you. That image is put together by what you have said in praise of me or to insult me, what you have done to me —it is put together by all the memories I have of you—and your image of me is put together in the same way, and it is those images which have relationship and which prevent us from really communing with each other.

一步，那第一步即是永恒的一步。

假如说你在独自散步，或是与人同行，然后你们停止了交谈。你被大自然所环绕，没有犬吠，没有汽车经过的噪声，甚至没有鸟儿振翅飞过。你完全安静下来，周围的大自然也寂静一片。在观察者与所观之物都十分宁静的状态中，观察者不再把他所观察到的转换成思想，在那份寂静中，就会出现一种截然不同的美。此时既没有自然，也没有观察者，只有一份完全、彻底独立的心境。心孑然独立于寂静之中——但不是孤立——那份寂静便是美。当你爱着，还会有观察者吗？只有当爱变成了欲望与快感，观察者才会出现。当欲望和快感与爱撇清了干系，此时的爱才是炽烈的，它就像美一样，每天都是崭新的。正如我所说，它既没有今日，也没有明天。

只有当我们不带任何先入之见、任何意象地去看，我们方能直接触及生命中的一切。我们所有的人际关系实际上都是虚构出来的，也就是说，是基于思想所构建的意象之上的。如果我对你抱有意象，你对我也抱有意象，我们自然就完全看不到真实的对方。我们见到的是我们为彼此构建的形象，而它们妨碍了真实的接触，这就是为什么我们的人际关系会出问题的原因。

当我说我了解你，我的意思其实是了解昨天的你。我实际上并不了解此刻的你，我所了解的只是我对你的印象。这个印象由你对我的赞扬或是侮辱，以及你对我所做的事拼凑而成，由我对你的所有记忆集结而成，你对我的印象也是如此形成的。是这些印象之间发生了关系，进而妨碍了我们与彼此产生真正的交流。

Two people who have lived together for a long time have an image of each other which prevents them from really being in relationship. If we understand relationship we can co-operate but co-operation cannot possibly exist through images, through symbols, through ideological conceptions. Only when we understand the true relationship between each other is there a possibility of love, and love is denied when we have images. Therefore it is important to understand, not intellectually but actually in your daily life, how you have built images about your wife, your husband, your neighbour, your child, your country, your leaders, your politicians, your gods—you have nothing but images.

These images create the space between you and what you observe and in that space there is conflict, so what we are going to find out now together is whether it is possible to be free of the space we create, not only outside ourselves but in ourselves, the space which divides people in all their relationships.

Now the very attention you give to a problem is the energy that solves that problem. When you give your complete attention—I mean with everything in you—there is no observer at all. There is only the state of attention which is total energy, and that total energy is the highest form of intelligence. Naturally that state of mind must be completely silent and that silence, that stillness, comes when there is total attention, not disciplined stillness. That total silence in which there is neither the observer nor the thing observed is the highest form of a religious mind. But what takes place in that state cannot be put into words because what is said in words is not the fact. To find out for yourself you have to go through it.

Every problem is related to every other problem so that if you can solve one problem completely—it does not matter what it is—you will

两个长久生活在一起的人，会对彼此产生印象，而这妨碍了他们建立真正的关系。如果我们懂得了关系这个问题，便能够彼此合作，但合作是不可能通过意象、符号以及意识形态上的观念来实现的。只有当我们懂得了彼此之间关系的真谛，才可能有爱，而当我们抱有意象时，爱就被否定了。因此重要的是了解——并非从智力上，而是在你的日常生活中真正去理解——你是如何为你的妻子、丈夫、邻居、孩子、国家、领袖、政客以及神明塑造意象的，除了一堆意象你一无所有。

这些意象造成了你与观察对象之间的空隙，那个空隙当中就有着冲突。因此我们现在要一起去弄清楚，有没有可能摆脱我们制造的这个空隙，不仅仅在我们之外，也包括在我们内心，那个在人际关系中造成分裂的空隙。

而你对一个问题所给予的关注，本身即是解决问题的能量。当你付出你全部的注意力——也就是付出你的一切——观察者便彻底消失了。只剩下这种全神贯注的状态，也就是完整的能量，这股完整的能量即是最高形式的智慧。毫无疑问，那样的心必须是完全沉静的，当你全神贯注时，那份寂静、那份安宁才会到来，但那不是修炼而来的安宁。在那份全然的寂静中，既无观察者，亦无所观之物，那即是最高形式的宗教之心。然而，那样的状态中所发生的事无法诉诸言语，因为文字所说的并非事实本身。若要亲自探明真相，你就必须亲身经历它。

所有的问题都是息息相关的，因此，你若能彻底解决一个问

see that you are able to meet all other problems easily and resolve them. We are talking, of course, of psychological problems. We have already seen that a problem exists only in time, that is when we meet the issue incompletely. So not only must we be aware of the nature and structure of the problem and see it completely, but meet it as it arises and resolve it immediately so that it does not take root in the mind. If one allows a problem to endure for a month or a day, or even for a few minutes, it distorts the mind. So is it possible to meet a problem immediately without any distortion and be immediately, completely, free of it and not allow a memory, a scratch on the mind, to remain? These memories are the images we carry about with us and it is these images which meet this extraordinary thing called life and therefore there is a contradiction and hence conflict. Life is very real—life is not an abstraction—and when you meet it with images there are problems.

Is it possible to meet every issue without this space-time interval, without the gap between oneself and the thing of which one is afraid? It is possible only when the observer has no continuity, the observer who is the builder of the image, the observer who is a collection of memories and ideas, who is a bundle of abstractions.

When you look at the stars there is you who are looking at the stars in the sky; the sky is flooded with brilliant stars, there is cool air, and there is you, the observer, the experiencer, the thinker, you with your aching heart, you, the centre, creating space. You will never understand about the space between yourself and the stars, yourself and your wife or husband, or friend, because you have never looked without the image, and that is why you do not know what beauty is or what love is. You talk about it, you write about it, but you have never known it except perhaps at rare intervals of total self-abandonment. So long as there is a centre creating space around

题——是什么问题无关紧要——你便会发现，你能够轻而易举地面对并解决其他所有的问题。当然，我们所说的是心理层面的问题。我们已然看清问题只存在于时间当中，也就是我们没有彻底面对问题之时。因此，我们不仅必须觉察问题的本质与结构，彻底看清它，而且在它崭露头角之时，就面对并即刻解决它，不让它在心中生根。如果你让问题持续一个月、一天，或者哪怕只有几分钟，它都会扭曲心灵。因此，有没有可能毫无扭曲地即刻面对问题，并且即刻彻底地摆脱它，不让任何记忆或是痕迹留在心中？那些记忆即是我们随身携带的印象，是这些印象在面对"人生"这件非凡的事，因而就有了矛盾以及冲突。生活是非常真实的——生活并非抽象的事物——当你用意象来面对它，问题便会在所难免。

有没有可能面对每一个问题，没有这种时空间隔，也没有一个人与他所恐惧的事物之间的隔阂？只有观察者不再延续——观察者即是意象的缔造者、记忆与观念的集合，以及堆积起来的抽象概念——那才是可能的。

当你凝望繁星，有一个"你"在看着天上的星斗。天幕缀满闪亮的星辰，空气凉爽，有一个"你"，这个观察者、体验者、思考者，带着自己伤痛的心，正是"你"，这个中心，制造了距离。你永远无法理解你与星辰之间的距离，你与你的妻子、丈夫、朋友之间的距离，因为你从未摆脱意象去看，那就是你为什么不明白何为美、何为爱的原因。你谈论爱，抒写爱，但你从未真正懂得它，也许除了鲜有的一些完全忘我的片刻。只要存在一个围绕自己制造空隙的中心，便

itself there is neither love nor beauty. When there is no centre and no circumference then there is love. And when you love you are beauty.

When you look at a face opposite, you are looking from a centre and the centre creates the space between person and person, and that is why our lives are so empty and callous. You cannot cultivate love or beauty, nor can you invent truth, but if you are all the time aware of what you are doing, you can cultivate awareness and out of that awareness you will begin to see the nature of pleasure, desire and sorrow and the utter loneliness and boredom of man, and then you will begin to come upon that thing called "the space".

When there is space between you and the object you are observing you will know there is no love, and without love, however hard you try to reform the world or bring about a new social order or however much you talk about improvements, you will only create agony. So it is up to you. There is no leader, there is no teacher, there is nobody to tell you what to do. You are alone in this mad brutal world.

既没有爱也没有美。当中心与外围都不复存在，爱才会出现。而你若爱着，你便是美。

当你看着对面的脸庞，你是从一个中心去看的，那个中心造成了人与人之间的距离，这就是我们的生命为什么如此空洞冷漠的原因。你无法培育爱或者美，你也无法发明真理。但是，如果你始终明了自己在做什么，你便可以培养觉察。从那份觉察中，你开始看清快感、欲望与悲伤的本质，以及人类极端的无聊与寂寞，此时你便可以懂得那个所谓"空隙"问题了。

当你和你所观察的对象之间有了空隙，你便知道爱已不在。没有了爱，无论你多么努力地改革世界、树立社会新秩序，也无论你对进步怎样高谈阔论，都只会招来痛苦。因此这取决于你。没有领袖，没有导师，没有人能告诉你该怎么办。在这个疯狂残忍的世界上，你孑然一身。

PART 12
第十二部分

The Observer and the Observed

观察者与被观察者

Please go on with me a little further. It may be rather complex, rather subtle, but please go on with it.

Now, when I build an image about you or about anything, I am able to watch that image, so there is the image and the observer of the image. I see someone, say, with a red shirt on and my immediate reaction is that I like it or that I don't like it. The like or dislike is the result of my culture, my training, my associations, my inclinations, my acquired and inherited characteristics. It is from that centre that I observe and make my judgement, and thus the observer is separate from the thing he observes.

But the observer is aware of more than one image; he creates thousands of images. But is the observer different from these images? Isn't he just another image? He is always adding to and subtracting from what he is; he is a living thing all the time weighing, comparing, judging, modifying and changing as a result of pressures from outside and within—living in the field of consciousness which is his own knowledge, influence and innumerable calculations. At the same time when you look at the observer, who is yourself, you see that he is made up of memories, experiences, accidents, influences, traditions and infinite varieties of suffering, all of which are the past. So the observer is both the past and the present, and tomorrow is waiting and that is also a part of him. He is half alive and half dead and with this death and life he is looking, with the dead and living leaf. And in that state of mind which is within the field of time, you (the

请一起与我再走一程。这段旅程也许看起来非常复杂、非常微妙，但还是请继续探索下去。

当我为你或是为任何事塑造了形象，我是可以观察那个形象的，因此既有形象，又有形象的观察者。比如说，见到有个人穿着红衬衫，我立刻做出了反应：喜欢或是不喜欢。这种好恶是我的文化、我的教养、我的联想、我的倾向、我后天习得与先天继承的性格的产物。它来自我进行观察和做出评判的那个中心，因而观察者与他所观之物割裂了开来。

但那个观察者发现远不止一个形象，他编织了数千个形象。可观察者有异于这些形象吗？他难道就不是另一个形象吗？他总是对自己真实的样子加加减减，他是一个活跃的存在，不停地权衡、比较、评判、修补以及改变，那都是外在与内心压力的结果。他活在意识的领域当中，而意识就是他自己的知识、他所受的影响，以及不计其数的算计。与此同时，当你看着观察者，也就是你自己，你会发现他是由各种记忆、经验、事件、影响、传统和无尽的苦难构成的，那一切都属于过去。所以观察者既是过去也是现在，而等候在那里的明天，也是他的一部分。他一半活着，一半已经死了，他就是在这种半死不活的状态下，透过已然死去和依然活着的片段去观察的。在这种受困于

observer) look at fear, at jealousy, at war, at the family (that ugly enclosed entity called the family) and try to solve the problem of the thing observed which is the challenge, the new; you are always translating the new in terms of the old and therefore you are everlastingly in conflict.

One image, as the observer, observes dozens of other images around himself and inside himself, and he says,"I like this image, I'm going to keep it" or "I don't like that image so I'll get rid of it", but the observer himself has been put together by the various images which have come into being through reaction to various other images. So we come to a point where we can say, "The observer is also the image, only he has separated himself and observes. This observer who has come into being through various other images thinks himself permanent and between himself and the images he has created there is a division, a time interval. This creates conflict between himself and the images he believes to be the cause of his troubles. So then he says, 'I must get rid of this conflict', but the very desire to get rid of the conflict creates another image."

Awareness of all this, which is real meditation, has revealed that there is a central image put together by all the other images, and the central image, the observer, is the censor, the experiencer, the evaluator, the judge who wants to conquer or subjugate the other images or destroy them altogether. The other images are the result of judgements, opinions and conclusions by the observer, and the observer is the result of all the other images—therefore the observer is the observed.

So awareness has revealed the different states of one's mind, has revealed the various images and the contradiction between the images, has revealed the resulting conflict and the despair at not being able to do anything about it and the various attempts to escape from it. All this has

时间领域的心态下，你（观察者）去看恐惧、嫉妒、战争、家庭（这个叫作"家庭"的丑陋封闭的实体），试图解决所观之物的问题——那崭新的挑战。你总是按照旧有的一套来诠释新生事物，因而必将永无止境地身陷冲突。

一个意象，也就是观察者，观察到周围以及自己内心有无数个其他的意象，于是说："我喜欢这个形象，我要留着它"，或者"我不喜欢那个形象，所以我要扔掉它"。但观察者本身正是由各种意象构成的，这些意象恰恰源于对其他各个意象产生的反应。所以到了这一步，我们可以说："观察者也是意象，只不过他先把自己分离了出来，然后再去观察。这个观察者脱胎于各种其他的意象，他以为自己是永恒的，于是他与他所编织的意象之间便产生了一种分别、一个时间间隔。这导致了他与意象之间的冲突，他认为这正是他各种麻烦的肇因。于是他说：'我必须消除这个冲突'，但消除冲突的愿望本身又制造了另外一个意象。"

觉察到这一切，即是真正的冥想，这揭示出了存在一个由其他意象所构成的核心意象，这个核心的意象，这个观察者，就是审查者、经验者、评估者，就是那个希望征服、镇压其他意象或是将它们一举摧毁的审判者。其他的意象皆是观察者的各种评判、观点和结论的产物，而观察者又是所有其他意象的产物，因此观察者正是被观察者。

因此觉察揭示了一个人的各种心智状态，揭示了各种意象以及意象之间的矛盾，揭示了随之而来的冲突、完全无能为力的绝望，以及各种从中逃离的企图。这一切都在小心谨慎的觉察中得以揭示，进而

been revealed through cautious hesitant awareness, and then comes the awareness that the observer is the observed. It is not a superior entity who becomes aware of this, it is not a higher self (the superior entity, the higher self, are merely inventions, further images); it is the awareness itself which had revealed that the observer is the observed.

If you ask yourself a question, who is the entity who is going to receive the answer? And who is the entity who is going to enquire? If the entity is part of consciousness, part of thought, then it is incapable of finding out. What it can find out is only a state of awareness. But if in that state of awareness there is still an entity who says, "I must be aware, I must practise awareness", that again is another image.

This awareness that the observer is the observed is not a process of identification with the observed. To identify ourselves with something is fairly easy. Most of us identify ourselves with something—with our family, our husband or wife, our nation—and that leads to great misery and great wars. We are considering something entirely different and we must understand it not verbally but in our core, right at the root of our being. In ancient China before an artist began to paint anything—a tree, for instance—he would sit down in front of it for days, months, years, it didn't matter how long, until he was the tree. He did not identify himself with the tree but he was the tree. This means that there was no space between him and the tree, no space between the observer and the observed, no experiencer experiencing the beauty, the movement, the shadow, the depth of a leaf, the quality of colour. He was totally the tree, and in that state only could he paint.

Any movement on the part of the observer, if he has not realized that the observer is the observed, creates only another series of images and again he is caught in them. But what takes place when the observer is aware

有了这份觉知：观察者即被观察者。并非一个高高在上的存在觉察到了这些，也不是一个什么"高我"（高高在上的存在、"高我"都不过是些发明，是另外一些意象罢了），而是觉察本身揭开了"观察者即被观察者"的真相。

如果你问了自己一个问题，谁是那个要去接收答案的实体呢？要去探索的那个实体又是谁？如果那个实体是意识的一部分、思想的一部分，那么它是无法找到真相的。它能找到的只是一种觉知的状态。但是，倘若那个觉知状态当中还有一个实体在说："我必须觉察，我必须练习觉察"，那么它就又成了另外一个意象。

对"观察者即被观察者"的这份觉知，并非一个对被观察者的认同过程。我们非常容易让自己认同某种东西，我们大多数人都与某些东西相认同——我们的家庭、丈夫、妻子以及国家——而那导致了深重的苦难与浩大的战争。我们所探究的是截然不同的事物，我们必须从我们存在的核心及根本上理解这一点，而不是从字面上去理解。中国古代的艺术家，在开始作画之前——比如说画一棵树——会在树跟前坐上数天、数月甚至数年，坐多久不重要，直到他成为那棵树。他并不是让自己认同那棵树，而是他就是那棵树。也就是说他与树之间没有距离，没有观察者与被观察者之间的空隙，没有一个体验者在体验那棵树的美、动态、叶片的深邃以及色彩的质地。他完完全全就是那棵树，在那样的状态之下他方能作画。

如果没有认识到观察者即被观察者，那么观察者一方的任何活动，都只会树立另一套意象，并再次困在其中。然而，当观察者觉察

that the observer is the observed? Go slowly, go very slowly, because it is a very complex thing we are going into now. What takes place? The observer does not act at all. The observer has always said, "I must do something about these images, I must suppress them or give them a different shape"; he is always active in regard to the observed, acting and reacting passionately or casually, and this action of like and dislike on the part of the observer is called positive action— "I like, therefore I must hold. I dislike therefore I must get rid of." But when the observer realizes that the thing about which he is acting is himself, then there is no conflict between himself and the image. He is that. He is not separate from that. When he was separate, he did, or tried to do, something about it, but when the observer realizes that he is that, then there is no like or dislike and conflict ceases.

For what is he to do? If something is you, what can you do? You cannot rebel against it or run away from it or even accept it. It is *there*. So all action that is the outcome of reaction to like and dislike has come to an end.

Then you will find that there is an awareness that has become tremendously alive. It is not bound to any central issue or to any image— and from that intensity of awareness there is a different quality of attention and therefore the mind—because the mind is this awareness—has become extraordinarily sensitive and highly intelligent.

到"观察者即被观察者"，那又会怎样？慢慢来，慢慢地往前走，因为现在我们探讨的是一件非常复杂的事。会发生什么？观察者根本不会有任何动作。观察者之前一直说："我必须对这些意象做点儿什么，我必须压制它们，或者把它们变成另一番样子。"他总是对被观察者跃跃欲试，或热情或随意地做出行动和反应。观察者做出的这种喜欢与否的行动就是所谓"积极的行动"——"我喜欢，所以我必须留住它。我不喜欢，所以我必须除掉它。"但是，当观察者认识到他行动的对象就是他自己，此时他与意象之间的冲突便消失了。他就是那个东西，他与意象没有分别。当二者分离开来，他便会对意象有所作为，或者起码试图做些什么。然而，当观察者领悟到他即是意象，此时便没有了好恶，冲突也随即止息了。

毕竟，他能做什么呢？如果某个东西就是你，你还能做什么吗？你无法反抗它、逃避它，你甚至都无法接受它，它就在**那里**。因此，所有的行动——也就是对好恶做出反应的结果——到此全部告终。

此时你便会发现，一份活力无限的觉察出现了，它不受制于任何重大事件或是任何意象。从那份强烈的觉察当中，便涌现了另一种品质的关注，进而心灵——因为心即是这份觉察——变得格外敏锐以及高度智慧。

PART 13
第十三部分

What is Thinking?—Ideas and Action—Challenge—Matter—The Beginning of Thought

何为思想？——观念与行动——挑战——物质——思想的开端

Let us now go into the question of what is thinking, the significance of that thought which must be exercised with care, logic and sanity (for our daily work) and that which has no significance at all. Unless we know the two kinds, we cannot possibly understand something much deeper which thought cannot touch. So let us try to understand this whole complex structure of what is thinking, what is memory, how thought originates, how thought conditions all our actions; and in understanding all this we shall perhaps come across something which thought has never discovered, which thought cannot open the door to.

Why has thought become so important in all our lives—thought being ideas, being the response to the accumulated memories in the brain cells? Perhaps many of you have not even asked such a question before, or if you have you may have said, "It's of very little importance—what is important is emotion." But I don't see how you can separate the two. If thought doesn't give continuity to feeling, feeling dies very quickly. So why in our daily lives, in our grinding, boring, frightened lives, has thought taken on such inordinate importance? Ask yourself as I am asking myself—why is one a slave to thought—cunning, clever, thought which can organize, which can start things, which has invented so much, bred so many wars, created so much fear, so much anxiety, which is forever making images and chasing its own tail—thought which has enjoyed the pleasure of yesterday and given that pleasure continuity in the present and also in the future—

现在我们来探讨一下"何为思想"这个问题，以及思想的意义。一方面，在日常生活中，我们必须对思想加以谨慎、理智和清醒的运用，而另一方面它又毫无意义。除非我们懂得了这两种思想，否则我们不可能领会某种思想所无法触及的深邃事物。因此，我们来试着了解这整个复杂的结构：思想是什么，记忆是什么，思想是如何产生的，它又如何制约了我们所有的行动。在对这一切的了解当中，我们也许便会邂逅某样思想从未发现也无法通达的事物。

为什么思想在我们的生活中变得如此重要？——思想即是观念，即是对脑细胞所储存记忆的反应。可能你们当中的很多人以前甚至从未问过这样一个问题，或者即使问过，你可能也会说："思想没什么重要性，重要的是感受。"但我认为你是无法将两者分开的。如果思想不给感受以延续性，感受很快便会消失。所以，在我们的日常生活中，在我们备受折磨、乏味、恐惧的生活中，为什么思想占据了如此过分的重要性？在我自问的时候，你也问问你自己：为什么人成了思想的奴隶？——思想聪明、狡猾、擅长组织、构建，有无数发明，催生了无数战争、无数恐惧、无数焦虑，永远在塑造意象，像狗一样追逐着自己的尾巴，享受了昨天的快感，又把快感延续到现在以及将来；思想一直蠢蠢欲动、喋喋不休，一直在活动、构建、加加减减、

thought which is always active, chattering, moving, constructing, taking away, adding, supposing?

Ideas have become far more important to us than action—ideas so cleverly expressed in books by the intellectuals in every field. The more cunning, the more subtle, those ideas are the more we worship them and the books that contain them. We are those books, we are those ideas, so heavily conditioned are we by them. We are forever discussing ideas and ideals and dialectically offering opinions. Every religion has its dogma, its formula, its own scaffold to reach the gods, and when inquiring into the beginning of thought we are questioning the importance of this whole edifice of ideas. We have separated ideas from action because ideas are always of the past and action is always the present—that is, living is always the present. We are afraid of living and therefore the past, as ideas, has become so important to us.

It is really extraordinarily interesting to watch the operation of one's own thinking, just to observe how one thinks, where that reaction we call thinking, springs from. Obviously from memory. Is there a beginning to thought at all? If there is, can we find out its beginning—that is, the beginning of memory, because if we had no memory we would have no thought?

We have seen how thought sustains and gives continuity to a pleasure that we had yesterday and how thought also sustains the reverse of pleasure which is fear and pain, so the experiencer, who is the thinker, is the pleasure and the pain and also the entity who gives nourishment to the pleasure and pain. The thinker separates pleasure from pain. He doesn't see that in the very demand for pleasure he is inviting pain and fear. Thought in human relationships is always demanding pleasure which it covers by different words like loyalty, helping, giving, sustaining, serving. I wonder why we

假设不断。

对我们来说，观念已经变得远比行动重要，各个领域的知识分子，都在书本中聪明地表达了各种观念。那些观念越是机巧、越是微妙，我们便越是崇拜它们以及它们所在的书籍。我们就是那些书本，我们就是那些观念，我们受到了它们如此严重的制约。我们没完没了地讨论概念、理想，提出各种辩证的观点。每种宗教都有自己的教条、自己的模式，都有各自找到神明的舷梯。当我们探究思想的开端，我们质疑的是这整个庞大的观念体系的意义。我们把观念与行动分离开来，因为观念始终属于过去，而行动属于现在，也就是说，生活永远是属于现在的。我们害怕生活，因此过去——也就是各种观念——才变得对我们如此重要。

观察你自己思想的运作，观察你是如何思考的，以及我们称为"思想"的反应从何而来，真的非常有趣。它们显然来自记忆。思想的开端究竟是否存在？如果存在，我们能不能发现它的开端，也就是记忆的开端？因为如果没有记忆，我们也就没有思想。

我们已经看清思想是如何维系和延续昨日的快感，思想又是如何维系着快感的反面，也就是恐惧和痛苦的。因此，经验者，即思想者，他就是快乐和痛苦，他本身也是滋养苦与乐的那个实体。思想者把苦与乐分离开来，他没发现对快感的追求本身便会招来痛苦与恐惧。人际关系中的思想总是渴望得到快感，却用忠诚、助人、付出、支持、服务等各种名词来掩饰。我很好奇我们为什么总想服务他人？加油站也提供良好的服务。帮助、付出、服务，这些词是什么意思？

want to serve? The petrol station offers good service. What do those words mean, to help, to give, to serve? What is it all about? Does a flower full of beauty, light and loveliness say,"I am giving, helping, serving"? It is! And because it is not trying to do anything it covers the earth.

Thought is so cunning, so clever, that it distorts everything for its own convenience. Thought in its demand for pleasure brings its own bondage. Thought is the breeder of duality in all our relationships: there is violence in us which gives us pleasure but there is also the desire for peace, the desire to be kind and gentle. This is what is going on all the time in all our lives. Thought not only breeds this duality in us, this contradiction, but it also accumulates the innumerable memories we have had of pleasure and pain, and from these memories it is reborn. So thought is the past, thought is always old, as I have already said.

As every challenge is met in terms of the past—a challenge being always new—our meeting of the challenge will always be totally inadequate, hence contradiction, conflict and all the misery and sorrow we are heir to. Our little brain is in conflict whatever it does. Whether it aspires, imitates, conforms, suppresses, sublimates, takes drugs to expand itself—whatever it does—it is in a state of conflict and will produce conflict.

Those who think a great deal are very materialistic because thought is matter. Thought is matter as much as the floor, the wall, the telephone, are matter. Energy functioning in a pattern becomes matter. There is energy and there is matter. That is all life is. We may think thought is not matter but it is. Thought is matter as an ideology. Where there is energy it becomes matter. Matter and energy are interrelated. The one cannot exist without the other, and the more harmony there is between the two, the more balance, the more active the brain cells are. Thought has set up this pattern

它们都是怎么回事？一朵充满了美、光彩和亮丽的花会说"我在付出、帮助和服务"吗？可它就在做着这些！而正因为它是无心为之，所以才开满大地。

思想是如此狡猾、如此聪明，它为着自己的便利而扭曲了一切。思想在对快感的追逐中作茧自缚。思想是我们所有关系中二元对立的繁育者——我们身上既有带来快感的暴力，又有对和平、友善与温柔的渴望。这就是我们所有人的生活中一直在上演的事。思想不仅滋生了我们内心的这种二元性、这种矛盾，它也积累了我们对过往苦与乐的无数记忆，它正是从这些记忆中复活的。因此，正如我之前所说的，思想即是过去，思想始终是陈旧的。

由于所有的挑战都由过去来面对——而挑战总是新的——因此我们面对挑战的方式始终是完全不妥当的，因而矛盾、冲突以及所有的痛苦和悲伤，对我们而言是在劫难逃。我们狭小的头脑无论做什么，都会身陷冲突。无论它渴望、模仿、遵从、压抑、升华，还是服用迷幻药来扩展自己——无论它做什么——都依然处于冲突状态，并且会继续制造冲突。

那些思考甚多的人是非常物质化的，因为思想即是物质。思想是物质，就如同地板、墙壁、电话也是物质一样。以某种形式运行的能量会变成物质。既有能量，也有物质，所有的生命都是如此。我们也许认为思想不是物质，但它就是物质，思想是观念形式的物质。有能量的地方，就会产生物质。物质与能量息息相关，两者缺一，另一个便无法存在。两者之间越是和谐、越是平衡，脑细胞就越是活跃。思

of pleasure, pain, fear, and has been functioning inside it for thousands of years and cannot break the pattern because it has created it.

A new fact cannot be seen by thought. It can be understood later by thought, verbally, but the understanding of a new fact is not reality to thought. Thought can never solve any psychological problem. However clever, however cunning, however erudite, whatever the structure thought creates through science, through an electronic brain, through compulsion or necessity, thought is never new and therefore it can never answer any tremendous question. The old brain cannot solve the enormous problem of living.

Thought is crooked because it can invent anything and see things that are not there. It can perform the most extraordinary tricks, and therefore it cannot be depended upon. But if you understand the whole structure of how you think, why you think, the words you use, the way you behave in your daily life, the way you talk to people, the way you treat people, the way you walk, the way you eat—if you are aware of all these things then your mind will not deceive you, then there is nothing to be deceived. The mind then is not something that demands, that subjugates; it becomes extraordinarily quiet, pliable, sensitive, alone, and in that state there is no deception whatsoever.

Have you ever noticed that when you are in a state of complete attention the observer, the thinker, the centre, the "me", comes to an end? In that state of attention thought begins to wither away.

If one wants to see a thing very clearly, one's mind must be very quiet, without all the prejudices, the chattering, the dialogue, the images, the pictures—all that must be put aside to look. And it is only in silence that you can observe the beginning of thought—not when you are searching, asking questions, waiting for a reply. So it is only when you are completely

想设下了快乐、痛苦和恐惧的模式，在其中运转了数千年，无法将模式打破，因为那正是它亲手塑造的。

思想无法看清新发的事实，它可以稍后从字面上加以理解，但对新事实的理解对思想来说并非真实。思想永远无法解决任何心理问题。无论思想如何聪明、如何狡猾、如何博学，无论思想借助科学、电脑、强制或是必要性搭建了怎样的结构，思想都绝不可能是新鲜的，因而它永远无法解答任何重大问题。陈旧的大脑无法解决生活这个巨大的难题。

思想是扭曲的，因为它擅长臆造和见到各种并不存在的事物。它会玩弄最不可思议的花招，因此完全不值得信赖。然而，如果你理解了这整个结构——你如何思考，你为何思考，你的用词，你日常生活中的行为方式，你如何与人讲话、如何对待他人，你如何走路、如何吃饭——如果你觉察到这一切，你的心便不会再欺骗你，也没什么可欺骗的对象。此时心不再渴求、不再征服，它变得无比安静、柔韧、敏感和独立，在那样的心境中任何欺骗都将不复存在。

你可曾注意到，当你处于全神贯注的状态，观察者、思想者，那个中心、那个"我"，便彻底止息了？在全神贯注的状态下，思想开始凋萎。

如果你想非常清晰地看到什么，你的心就必须非常安静，不带丝毫偏见、意象和画面，也没有喋喋不休、自言自语——那一切必须都抛开方能去看。只有在寂静中你方能观察思想的出现，而不是你追寻、提问、等待答案的时候。因此，只有当你彻底安静下来，从你存

quiet, right through your being, having put that question, "What is the beginning of thought?", that you will begin to see, out of that silence, how thought takes shape.

If there is an awareness of how thought begins then there is no need to control thought. We spend a great deal of time and waste a great deal of energy all through our lives, not only at school, trying to control our thoughts—"This is a good thought, I must think about it a lot. This is an ugly thought, I must suppress it." There is a battle going on all the time between one thought and another, one desire and another, one pleasure dominating all other pleasures. But if there is an awareness of the beginning of thought, then there is no contradiction in thought.

Now when you hear a statement like "Thought is always old" or "Time is sorrow", thought begins to translate it and interpret it. But the translation and interpretation are based on yesterday's knowledge and experience, so you will invariably translate according to your conditioning. But if you look at the statements and do not interpret them all but just give them your complete attention (not concentration) you will find there is neither the observer nor the observed, neither the thinker nor the thought. Don't say, "Which began first?" That is a clever argument which leads nowhere. You can observe in yourself that as long as there is no thought—which doesn't mean a state of amnesia, of blankness—as long as there is no thought derived from memory, experience or knowledge, which are all of the past, there is no thinker at all. This is not a philosophical or mystical affair. We are dealing with actual facts, and you will see, if you have gone this far in the journey, that you will respond to a challenge, not with the old brain, but totally anew.

在的最深处提出这个问题："思想从何处发端？"从那份寂静之中，你才能开始发现思想是如何成形的。

如果觉察到了思想是如何出现的，那么就没必要去控制思想了。不止在学生时代，我们的整个一生花掉了大量的时间，耗费了大量的精力，试图去控制我们的思想——"这是个好想法，我必须多想一想。那是个丑陋的念头，我必须压制它。"各个念头、各个欲望之间一直征战不休，一种快感主宰着其他的所有快感。然而，如果觉察到了思想的开端，思想之中的矛盾便将不复存在。

那么，当你听到了"思想始终是陈旧的"或者"时间即是悲伤"这样的表述，思想便会开始对它进行翻译和诠释。但翻译和诠释奠基于昨日的知识与经验，所以你的诠释必定受制于你的局限。但是，如果你看着这些表述却丝毫不做诠释，而只是付出你全然的关注（而非专注），你便会发现既无观察者，亦无被观察者，既无思想者，亦无思想。不要说："哪个在先？"那不过是个毫无助益的机巧说辞罢了。你可以在自己身上观察到这一点：只要没有思想——这并非指一种失忆或空白状态——只要没有脱胎于过往记忆、经验或知识的思想，思想者也就根本不会存在。这并非一件哲学上的或者神秘的事，我们探讨的是千真万确的事实。如果这段旅程你已走到此处，你便会发现，你不再用陈旧的头脑，而是会以全新的方式去应对挑战。

PART 14
第十四部分

In the life we generally lead there is very little solitude. Even when we are alone our lives are crowded by so many influences, so much knowledge, so many memories of so many experiences, so much anxiety, misery and conflict that our mind become duller and duller, more and more insensitive, functioning in a monotonous routine. Are we ever alone? Or are we carrying with us all the burdens of yesterday?

There is a rather nice story of two monks walking from one village to another and they come upon a young girl sitting on the bank of a river, crying. And one of the monks goes up to her and says, "Sister, what are you crying about?" She says, "You see that house over there across the river? I came over this morning early and had no trouble wading across but now the river has swollen and I can't get back. There is no boat." "Oh," says the monk, "that is no problem at all", and he picks her up and carries her across the river and leaves her on the other side. And the two monks go on together. After a couple of hours, the other monk says, "Brother, we have taken a vow never to touch a woman. What you have done is a terrible sin. Didn't you have pleasure, a great sensation, in touching a woman?" and the other monk replies, "I left her behind two hours ago. You are still carrying her, aren't you?"

That is what we do. We carry our burdens all the time; we never die to them, we never leave them behind. It is only when we give complete attention to a problem and solve it immediately—never carrying it over to the next day, the next minute—that there is solitude. Then, even, if we

在我们通常所过的生活中，独处极为难得。即使我们独自一人，生活中依然充斥着不计其数的影响、知识、对经验的记忆，以及如此之多的焦虑、痛苦与冲突，乃至我们的心变得越来越迟钝，越来越麻木，在千篇一律的常规中运转。我们可曾真正独处过？抑或，我们始终背负着昨日的累累重担？

有一个非常有趣的故事，讲的是两名僧人要从一个村子到另一个村子去，他们在路上遇到了一位坐在河边哭泣的年轻女子。其中一个僧人上前问道："这位姐妹，你为何哭泣？"她回答说："你看到河对岸那座房子了吗？我今天一大早涉水过来，没遇到任何麻烦，但现在河水涨高了，我回不去了，这儿又没有船。""噢，"僧人说，"这完全不是问题"，随后他背起女子过了河，把她放在了河对岸，然后两个僧人又继续往前走。过了几小时，另一个僧人说："师兄，我们曾经发过誓，绝不碰女人，你刚才所做的是一桩可怕的罪行。你碰那个女人的时候，难道没有快感，没有一种巨大的享受吗？"这位僧人回答道："两小时之前我就把她放下了，可你还在背着她，不是吗？"

这正是我们所做的事。我们时时刻刻背着包袱，从来没有对它们死去，从没把它们抛在身后。只有当我们全神贯注于一个问题，并且

live in a crowded house or are in a bus, we have solitude. And that solitude indicates a fresh mind, an innocent mind.

To have inward solitude and space is very important because it implies freedom to be, to go, to function, to fly. After all, goodness can only flower in space just as virtue can flower only when there is freedom. We may have political freedom but inwardly we are not free and therefore there is no space. No virtue, no quality that is worth while, can function or grow without this vast space within oneself. And space and silence are necessary because it is only when the mind is alone, uninfluenced, untrained, not held by infinite varieties of experience, that it can come upon something totally new.

One can see directly that it is only when the mind is silent that there is a possibility of clarity. The whole purpose of meditation in the East is to bring about such a state of mind—that is, to control thought, which is the same as constantly repeating a prayer to quieten the mind and in that state hoping to understand one's problems. But unless one lays the foundation, which is to be free from fear, free from sorrow, anxiety and all the traps one lays for oneself, I do not see how it is possible for a mind to be actually quiet. This is one of the most difficult things to communicate. Communication between us implies, doesn't it, that not only must you understand the words I am using but that we must both, you and I, be intense at the same time, not a moment later or a moment sooner and capable of meeting each other on the same level? And such communication is not possible when you are interpreting what you are reading according to your own knowledge, pleasure or opinions, or when you are making a tremendous effort to comprehend.

It seems to me that one of the greatest stumbling blocks in life is this constant struggle to reach, to achieve, to acquire. We are trained from

立刻将它解决，决不拖到下一天、下一分钟，才算是真正的独处。那样的话，即使住在拥挤的房间，或是置身巴士当中，我们依然是独自一人。而那份独处便意味着一颗清新、纯真的心。

享有内心的独立和空间至关重要，因为那意味着存在的自由、行动的自由、生活的自由以及翱翔的自由。毕竟，善只能在空间中绽放，正如美德也只能在自由中绽放。我们或许拥有政治上的自由，但我们内心并不自由，因而也没有空间。如果一个人内心没有这样广袤的空间，美德、宝贵的品质是不可能运行、成长的。空间和寂静是必不可少的，因为只有心孑然独立，未受影响，未被训诫，也没有受控于花样繁多的经验，才可能邂逅某种崭新之物。

我们可以直截了当地看到，心只有寂静时才可能是清明的。东方的冥想，其全部用意皆在于实现这样一种心灵状态——也就是去控制思想——而这跟不断复诵祈祷以期让内心安静，然后指望在那种状态下能够理解自身的问题，都是一回事。然而，除非我们打下基础，也就是从恐惧、悲伤、焦虑以及自设的所有陷阱中解脱出来，否则我认为心灵根本不可能真的寂静。这是最难沟通的事情之一。我们之间的沟通，意味着你不仅要理解我使用的字句，而且我们，你和我，必须同时抱有强烈的热情，不迟也不早，而是能够在同一个层面上彼此交会，不是吗？但是，当你按照自己的知识、喜好或是看法来诠释你读到的内容，或者非常努力地去理解时，那样的沟通便不可能发生了。

在我看来，人生最大的绊脚石之一，便是这种不断去达成、实现与获取的努力。我们从小所受的训练便是获取和实现——脑细胞本身

childhood to acquire and to achieve—the very brain cells themselves create and demand this pattern of achievement in order to have physical security, but psychological security is not within the field of achievement. We demand security in all our relationships, attitudes and activities but, as we have seen, there is actually no such thing as security. To find out for yourself that there is no form of security in any relationship - to realize that psychologically there is nothing permanent—gives a totally different approach to life. It is essential, of course, to have outward security - shelter, clothing, food—but that outward security is destroyed by the demand for psychological security.

Space and silence are necessary to go beyond the limitations of consciousness, but how can a mind which is so endlessly active in its self-interest be quiet? One can discipline it, control it, shape it, but such torture does not make the mind quiet; it merely makes it dull. Obviously the mere pursuit of the ideal of having a quiet mind is valueless because the more you force it the more narrow and stagnant it becomes. Control in any form, like suppression, produces only conflict. So control and outward discipline are not the way, nor has an undisciplined life any value.

Most of our lives are outwardly disciplined by the demands of society, by the family, by our own suffering, by our own experience, by conforming to certain ideological or factual patterns—and that form of discipline is the most deadening thing. Discipline must be without control, without suppression, without any form of fear. How is this discipline to come about? It is not discipline first and then freedom; freedom is at the very beginning, not at the end. To understand this freedom, which is the freedom from the conformity of discipline, is discipline itself. The very act of learning is discipline (after all the root meaning of the word discipline is to learn), the very act of learning

需要并创造出这种追求成就的模式，以便取得身体上的保障，但心理上的安全无法纳入追求的范畴。在所有的关系、立场和行为中，我们都想得到安全感，但正如我们所见，安全这回事实际上并不存在。亲自发现任何关系中都没有安全存在，认识到心理上没什么是永恒的，便会带来一种截然不同的人生态度。当然，外在的保障是必不可少的——住所、衣服和食物——但外在的保障已经被人们对心理安全的追求所摧毁。

要超越意识的局限，空间和寂静是必不可少的。然而，一颗永远在为自身利益蠢蠢欲动的心，怎么才能安静下来呢？你可以约束它、控制它、塑造它，但这种折磨并不会让心安静，而只会让它变得更加迟钝。单纯去追求"拥有一颗安静的心"这个理想，显然是毫无意义的，因为你越是强迫它，它就会变得越狭隘、越停滞。任何形式的控制，比如压抑，都只会造成冲突。因此控制与外在的戒律并非出路，而放纵无度的生活同样也毫无价值。

从外在来讲，我们的大部分生活都受制于社会的要求，受制于家庭，受制于我们自己的痛苦、自己的经验，以及对某些观念或现实模式的遵从，而任何形式的戒律都是最具破坏性的东西。纪律必须没有丝毫控制、丝毫压抑以及任何形式的恐惧。那么这种纪律如何才能产生？并不是先有纪律再有自由，自由就在起点，而非终点。了解这份自由，这份从对纪律的遵奉中解脱出来的自由，正是纪律本身。学习的行动本身便是纪律（说到底，"纪律"一词的词根义便是"学习"），学习的行动本身便会带来清明。若要了解控制、压抑与沉溺

becomes clarity. To understand the whole nature and structure of control, suppression and indulgence demands attention. You don't have to impose discipline in order to study it, but the very act of studying brings about its own discipline in which there is no suppression.

In order to deny authority (we are talking of psychological authority, not the law)—to deny the authority of all religious organizations, traditions and experience, one has to see why one normally obeys—actually study it. And to study it there must be freedom from condemnation, justification, opinion or acceptance. Now we cannot accept authority and yet study it—that is impossible. To study the whole psychological structure of authority within ourselves there must be freedom. And when we are studying we are denying the whole structure, and when we do deny, that very denial is the light of the mind that is free from authority. Negation of everything that has been considered worthwhile, such as outward discipline, leadership, idealism, is to study it; then that very act of studying is not only discipline but the negative of it, and the very denial is a positive act. So we are negating all those things that are considered important to bring about the quietness of the mind.

Thus we see it is not control that leads to quietness. Nor is the mind quiet when it has an object which is so absorbing that it gets lost in that object. This is like giving a child an interesting toy; he becomes very quiet, but remove the toy and he returns to his mischief-making. We all have our toys which absorb us and we think we are very quiet, but if a man is dedicated to a certain form of activity, scientific, literary or whatever it is, the toy merely absorbs him and he is not really quiet at all.

The only silence we know is the silence when noise stops, the silence when thought stops—but that is not silence. Silence is something entirely different, like beauty, like love. And this silence is not the product of a

的整个本质与结构，便需要全神贯注。若要学习，你无须强加戒律，而是学习的行动本身便会带来自身的纪律，其中却没有一丝压抑。

为了否定权威（我们谈的是精神权威，而不是法律），否定所有的宗教组织、传统和经验的权威，我们就必须看清人为什么通常会服从——实实在在地探究这一点。而要探究权威，就必须从谴责、辩解、观点或是接受中解脱出来。我们不能既接受权威同时又去探究它，那是不可能的。若要探究我们内在权威的整个心理结构，就必须具备自由。在探究的过程当中，我们就在否定这整个结构，当我们真的否定了它，那否定本身便是摆脱了权威的心灵之光。否定人们认为有价值的一切，比如，外在的戒律、领导和理想主义，便是去探究它。这种探究的行动本身就不仅仅是纪律，而且是对探究对象的否定，这份否定本身便是一种肯定的行动。因此，我们是在否定人们认为对带来心灵寂静而言重要的一切。

这样我们就看清了通往寂静的并非控制。而当有一件引人入胜的事，心完全沉迷其中的时候，心也不是安静的。那就像是给了孩子一个有趣的玩具，他变得非常安静，但是拿走了那个玩具，他就会再次顽皮起来。我们都有吸引自己的玩具，我们认为自己很安静，然而，即使一个人献身于某种形式的活动，无论是科学、文学还是别的什么活动，那件玩具也不过是暂时吸引了他，他根本不是真的安静。

我们所知的唯一寂静，是声音止息时的寂静，是念头停下时的寂静，但那并非真正的寂静。寂静是截然不同的东西，正如美，正如爱。这寂静也不是一颗安静的头脑的产物，并非脑细胞明白了那整个

quiet mind, it is not the product of the brain cells which have understood the whole structure and say, "For God's sake be quiet"; then the brain cells themselves produce the silence and that is not silence. Nor is silence the outcome of attention in which the observer is the observed; then there is no friction, but that is not silence.

You are waiting for me to describe what this silence is so that you can compare it, interpret it, carry it away and bury it. It cannot be described. What can be described is the known, and the freedom from the known can come into being only when there is a dying every day to the known, to the hurts, the flatteries, to all the images you have made, to all your experiences— dying every day so that the brain cells themselves become fresh, young, innocent. But that innocency, that freshness, that quality of tenderness and gentleness, does not produce love; it is not the quality of beauty or silence.

That silence which is not the silence of the ending of noise is only a small beginning. It is like going through a small hole to an enormous, wide, expansive ocean, to an immeasurable, timeless state. But this you cannot understand verbally unless you have understood the whole structure of consciousness and the meaning of pleasure, sorrow and despair, and the brain cells themselves have become quiet. Then perhaps you may come upon that mystery which nobody can reveal to you and nothing can destroy. A living mind is a still mind, a living mind is a mind that has no centre and therefore no space and time. Such a mind is limitless and that is the only truth, that is the only reality.

结构，然后说："看在老天的分上安静下来吧！"此时脑细胞自己制造出来的安静，并非真正的寂静。寂静也不是观察者与所观之物合一的关注状态的结果，此时虽没有冲突，但那也不是寂静。

你在等我来描述寂静是什么，这样你就可以比较它、诠释它，把它带走然后埋起来。但它无法描述，能够描述的都是已知。只有当你每天都对已知，对各种伤害和奉承，对你塑造的所有形象、所有经验统统死去，方能从已知中解脱出来——每天都彻底死去，这样脑细胞才会变得清新、年轻、纯真。但那份纯真，那份新鲜，那份温柔友善的品质，并不会产生爱，那还不是美或寂静的品质。

那份并非声音止息的寂静仅仅是个小小的开端，就像是穿过一个小孔，方能进入一片浩瀚、宽阔、广袤的海洋，进入一种不可估量的、超越时间的状态。但你无法通过言语理解这一点，除非你了悟了意识的整个结构，以及快乐、悲伤与绝望的含义，进而脑细胞本身变得安静下来。此时你或许便能偶遇那个无人能揭开，也没什么能毁灭的奥秘。一颗生机勃发的心是一颗宁静的心，是一颗没有中心进而时空也消失了的心。这样的一颗心是无限的，而这便是唯一的真理，唯一的真相。

PART 15
第十五部分

Experience—Satisfaction—Duality—Meditation

经验——满足感——二元性——冥想

We all want experiences of some kind—the mystical experience, the religious experience, the sexual experience, the experience of having a great deal of money, power, position, domination. As we grow older we may have finished with the demands of our physical appetites but then we demand wider, deeper and more significant experiences, and we try various means to obtain them—expanding our consciousness, for instance, which is quite an art, or taking various kinds of drugs. This is an old trick which has existed from time immemorial—chewing a piece of leaf or experimenting with the latest chemical to bring about a temporary alteration in the structure of the brain cells, a greater sensitivity and heightened perception which give a semblance of reality. This demand for more and more experiences shows the inward poverty of man. We think that through experiences we can escape from ourselves but these experiences are conditioned by what we are. If the mind is petty, jealous, anxious, it may take the very latest form of drug but it will still see only its own little creation, its own little projections from its own conditioned background.

Most of us demand completely satisfying, lasting experiences which cannot be destroyed by thought. So behind this demand for experience is the desire for satisfaction, and the demand for satisfaction dictates the experience, and therefore we have not only to understand this whole business of satisfaction but also the thing that is experienced. To have some great satisfaction is a great pleasure; the more lasting, deep and wide

我们都希望获得某种经验——神秘经验、宗教经验、性经验，以及拥有大量金钱、权力、地位和掌控的经验。随着年纪增长，我们也许满足了身体上的需求，但随后我们便想获得更广、更深、更重大的经验，并且尝试各种手段去得到它们，比如说，扩展意识——那可真是门"艺术"——或者服用各种药物。这是个自远古就已经存在的把戏了——嚼片叶子或是拿最新的化学物质做实验，为脑细胞的结构带来短暂的改变，带来更高的敏锐度和觉察力，进而貌似窥见了真相。对越来越多经验的这种渴望，表明了人内心的贫乏。我们以为借助各种经验即可逃离自己，但这些经验偏偏受制于我们此刻的自己。如果心狭隘、嫉妒、焦虑，即使服下最时新的迷幻药，它见到的依然只是自己从局限的背景中捏造和投射出来的琐屑罢了。

我们大多数人都渴望得到使人完全满足而又持久的经验——思想也无法将其败坏。因此，这种对经验的需求背后是对满足感的渴望，这份渴望掌控了经验，所以我们必须既了解满足感的来龙去脉，也要了解所体验到的事物。享受巨大的满足是一种极大的快感，体验越久、越深、越广，快感就越强烈，因此快感支配着我们所期望经验的形式，快感便是我们衡量经验的标尺。然而，任何可衡量的事物都在思想的局限之内，进而必定会制造幻觉。你可以拥有不可思议的经

the experience the more pleasurable it is, so pleasure dictates the form of experience we demand, and pleasure is the measure by which we measure the experience. Anything measurable is within the limits of thought and is apt to create illusion. You can have marvellous experiences and yet be completely deluded. You will inevitably see visions according to your conditioning; you will see Christ or Buddha or whoever you happen to believe in, and the greater a believer you are the stronger will be your visions, the projections of your own demands and urges.

So if in seeking something fundamental, such as what is truth, pleasure is the measure, you have already projected what that experience will be and therefore it is no longer valid.

What do we mean by experience? Is there anything new or original in experience? Experience is a bundle of memories responding to a challenge and it can respond only according to its background, and the cleverer you are at interpreting the experience the more it responds. So you have to question not only the experience of another but your own experience. If you don't recognize an experience it isn't an experience at all. Every experience has already been experienced or you wouldn't recognize it. You recognize an experience as being good, bad, beautiful, holy and so on according to your conditioning, and therefore the recognition of an experience must inevitably be old.

When we demand an experience of reality—as we all do, don't we?— to experience it we must know it and the moment we recognise it we have already projected it and therefore it is not real because it is still within the field of thought and time. If thought can think about reality it cannot be reality. We cannot recognize a new experience. It is impossible. We recognize only something we have already known and therefore when we say we have

验，但依然完全蒙在鼓里。你不可避免地会见到各种景象，那都源于你的局限，你会见到基督、佛陀或者你信奉的任何对象，并且你越是坚信，你的幻象，你自身欲求与渴望的化身便会越清晰。

因此，在探究某些根本问题时，比如，何为真理，倘若快感是衡量的尺度，你便已经投射出了经验的轮廓，因而那些经验便不再可取。

我们所说的"经验"是何含义？经验当中有任何崭新或是原初的东西吗？经验不过是一堆记忆在应对挑战，它只能根据自己的背景做出反应，而在诠释经验方面你越是聪明，做出的反应就会越多。因此，你不仅要质疑他人的经验，也必须质疑自己的经验。如果你没有认出一个经验，那它就根本不成其为经验。所有的经验都已然被经历过，否则你便不会认出它。囿于你所受的制约，你才认出某个经验是好的、坏的、美的、神圣的等，因此经验一经识别，便不可避免地是陈旧的。

当我们渴望经历真相——我们都希望如此，不是吗？——要经历它，我们就必须认得它。而一旦认出了它，我们就已经投射了它，所以那并非真相，因为它依然在思想与时间的领域之内。如果思想可以思考真相，那便不可能是真相。我们无法认出一个新经验，那是不可能的。我们只能认出已经知道的东西，因此，当我们说自己有了一次新体验，它根本就不是新的。通过意识扩展——正如人们借助各种迷幻药所做的那样——来寻求更多的经验，那依然属于意识的范畴，因而是非常局限的。

因此，我们发现了一个根本的真相，那就是：一颗在寻求、在渴

had a new experience it is not new at all. To seek further experience through expansion of consciousness, as is being done through various psychedelic drugs, is still within the field of consciousness and therefore very limited.

So we have discovered a fundamental truth, which is that a mind that is seeking, craving, for wider and deeper experience is a very shallow and dull mind because it lives always with its memories.

Now if we didn't have any experience at all, what would happen to us? We depend on experiences, on challenges, to keep us awake. If there were no conflicts within ourselves, no changes, no disturbances, we would all be fast asleep. So challenges are necessary for most of us; we think that without them our minds will become stupid and heavy, and therefore we depend on a challenge, an experience, to give us more excitement, more intensity, to make our minds sharper. But in fact this dependence on challenges and experiences to keep us awake, only makes our minds duller—it doesn't really keep us awake at all. So I ask myself, is it possible to keep awake totally, not peripherally at a few points of my being, but totally awake without any challenge or any experience? This implies a great sensitivity, both physical and psychological; it means I have to be free of all demands, for the moment I demand I will experience. And to be free of demand and satisfaction necessitates investigation into myself and an understanding of the whole nature of demand.

Demand is born out of duality: "I am unhappy and I must be happy". In that very demand that I must be happy is unhappiness. When one makes an effort to be good, in that very goodness is its opposite, evil. Everything affirmed contains its own opposite, and effort to overcome strengthens that against which it strives. When you demand an experience of truth or reality, that very demand is born out of your discontent with what is, and therefore the demand creates the opposite. And in the opposite there is what has

望更广、更深经验的心，是一颗非常肤浅、非常呆板的心，因为它一直活在自己的回忆里。

那么，如果我们根本没有丝毫经验，那又会怎样？我们仰仗经验、仰仗挑战来让自己保持清醒。如果内心没有冲突、没有变化、没有打扰，我们很快都会昏昏睡去。所以对我们大多数人来说，挑战是必不可少的。我们以为如果没有挑战，我们的心就会变得愚蠢、笨重，于是我们依赖挑战和经验带来更多的刺激、更多的热情，让我们的心更为敏锐。但事实上，这种依赖挑战和经验让自己清醒的做法，只会让我们的心更加迟钝，那实际上根本不会让我们清醒。因此我问自己：有没有可能完全保持清醒，并非在生活的边边角角，而是全然清醒，却无须任何挑战或是经验？这意味着身体上、心理上都拥有极高的敏锐度，意味着我必须摆脱所有欲求，因为一旦我有所求，经验便会接踵而至。而若要摆脱欲求以及满足感，就亟须探究我自己，亟须了解欲求的整个本质。

欲求脱胎于二元性："我不快乐，但我必须快乐。"这个"我必须快乐"的欲求本身之中就包含了不快乐。当一个人努力变得善良，那种善良当中就蕴含着它的反面——邪恶。所有决心当中都包含着它自身的对立面，努力去克服什么，反而会加强你拼命对抗的东西。当你渴望体验真理或是真相，那个欲求本身便脱胎于你对现实的不满，进而制造了对立面，而那个对立面当中便包含着既存的现实。因此，你必须摆脱这份无休止的欲求，否则二元对立的廊道将永无尽头。这实际上意味着你要彻底认清自己，乃至心绝不再追寻。

been. So one must be free of this incessant demand, otherwise there will be no end to the corridor of duality. This means knowing yourself so completely that the mind is no longer seeking.

Such a mind does not demand experience; it cannot ask for a challenge or know a challenge; it does not say, "I am asleep" or "I am awake". It is completely what it is. Only the frustrated, narrow, shallow mind, the conditioned mind, is always seeking the more. Is it possible then to live in this world without the more—without this everlasting comparison? Surely it is? But one has to find out for oneself.

Investigation into this whole question is meditation. That word had been used both in the East and the West in a most unfortunate way. There are different schools of meditation, different methods and systems. There are systems which say, "Watch the movement of your big toe, watch it, watch it, watch it"; there are other systems which advocate sitting in a certain posture, breathing regularly or practising awareness. All this is utterly mechanical. The other method gives you a certain word and tells you that if you go on repeating it you will have some extraordinary transcendental experience. This is sheer nonsense. It is a form of self-hypnosis. By repeating Amen or Om or Coca-Cola indefinitely you will obviously have a certain experience because by repetition the mind becomes quiet. It is a well known phenomenon which has been practised for thousands of years in India—Mantra Yoga it is called. By repetition you can induce the mind to be gentle and soft but it is still a petty, shoddy, little mind. You might as well put a piece of stick you have picked up in the garden on the mantelpiece and give it a flower every day. In a month you will be worshipping it and not to put a flower in front of it will become a sin.

Meditation is not following any system; it is not constant repetition and

这样的一颗心不再渴望经验，它不会邀约挑战，也不会认得挑战，它不会说"我睡着了"或是"我很清醒"，它完全就是此刻真实的自己。只有沮丧、狭隘、肤浅的心，只有局限的心总在追求更多。那么，有没有可能活在这个世界上，却不追求更多，也没有这种没完没了的比较？确实是可能的吗？但你得亲自去弄清楚这一点。

探究这整个问题，便是冥想。然而，这个名词在东西方都被以毁灭性的方式使用着。各式各样的冥想流派、方法和体系层出不穷。有些体系说："盯着你大脚趾的活动，一直看、一直看、一直看"；另一些体系则主张保持特定的坐姿，均匀地呼吸，或是练习觉知力。所有这些都机械无比。还有一类方法则给你一些字句，告诉你只要反复诵念，便会得到某些超凡入圣的奇妙体验。这完全是胡说八道，不过是一种自我催眠的手段罢了。无论是诵念"阿门""唵"，还是诵念"可口可乐"，显然你都必定会获得某种体验，因为借助复诵，心会变得安静。这是个人尽皆知的现象，在印度已经奉行了几千年，也就是所谓"曼陀罗瑜伽"。通过反复诵念，你可以让心变得温和柔软，但那依然是一颗琐碎、卑微、狭隘的心。另外，你还大可从花园里捡回一根木棒，把它放在壁炉上，每天奉上一枝花。一个月之后你就已经开始膜拜它了，若是不拿花朵来供奉它，那可就是罪过了。

冥想不是追随任何一种体系，也不是反复不停地诵念和模仿。冥想不是专注。坚持让弟子练习专注——也就是，让心专注一念，同时驱散其他所有的念头——是某些冥想大师最热衷的花招了。这是最为愚蠢和丑陋的事了，任何一个小学生被逼之下都会这么做。那意味着

imitation. Meditation is not concentration. It is one of the favourite gambits of some teachers of meditation to insist on their pupils learning concentration— that is, fixing the mind on one thought and driving out all other thoughts. This is a most stupid, ugly thing, which any schoolboy can do because he is forced to. It means that all the time you are having a battle between the insistence that you must concentrate on the one hand and your mind on the other which wanders away to all sorts of other things, whereas you should be attentive to every movement of the mind wherever it wanders. When your mind wanders off it means you are interested in something else.

Meditation demands an astonishingly alert mind; meditation is the understanding of the totality of life in which every form of fragmentation has ceased. Meditation is not control of thought, for when thought is controlled it breeds conflict in the mind, but when you understand the structure and origin of thought, which we have already been into, then thought will not interfere. That very understanding of the structure of thinking is its own discipline which is meditation.

Meditation is to be aware of every thought and of every feeling, never to say it is right or wrong but just to watch it and move with it. In that watching you begin to understand the whole movement of thought and feeling. And out of this awareness comes silence. Silence put together by thought is stagnation, is dead, but the silence that comes when thought has understood its own beginning, the nature of itself, understood how all thought is never free but always old—this silence is meditation in which the meditator is entirely absent, for the mind has emptied itself of the past.

If you have read this book for a whole hour attentively, that is meditation. If you have merely taken away a few words and gathered a few ideas to think about later, then it is no longer meditation. Meditation is a

你内心一直在交战，一方面你坚持必须集中注意力，另一方面你的心思早就跑到了其他各种事情上。你应该关注的是心的一举一动，无论它跑到了哪里。当你的心思游离开去，那就说明你感兴趣的是另外一些事情。

冥想需要一颗敏锐得惊人的心，冥想即是对生命整体的了悟，任何形式的分裂在其中都已偃旗息鼓。冥想并非控制思想，因为当思想受到了控制，便会在心中引发冲突。然而，当你理解了思想的结构与起源——这些我们都探讨过了——思想便不会再横加干涉。对思想结构的了解本身便是它自身的纪律，便是冥想。

冥想乃是觉知每一个想法、每一个感受，绝不说它是对是错，而只是看着它并随它而动。在那份观察中，你开始了解思想与感情的全部活动，从这份觉知中便会诞生寂静。思想所引发的寂静是停滞的、僵死的，但是，当思想懂得了自身的起源与本质，懂得了为何思想永远是陈旧的，绝不可能自由，寂静便会到来。这份寂静便是冥想，冥想者在其中完全缺席，因为心已然清空了过去。

如果你这一整小时都在全神贯注地读这本书，那就已经是冥想了。可如果你只是抽取其中的几句话，收集几个观点然后回头再去思考，那就不再是冥想了。冥想乃是这样一种心灵状态：它倾注全部的、完整的注意力——而非其中的一部分——去观察一切。但没人能教你如何全神贯注。如果有个体系教你如何全神贯注，那么你关注的就是那个体系，所以那不是冥想。冥想是生活中最伟大的艺术之一——也许就是最伟大的，没有之一——但你不可能从任何人那里

state of mind which looks at everything with complete attention, totally, not just parts of it. And no one can teach you how to be attentive. If any system teaches you how to be attentive, then you are attentive to the system and that is not attention. Meditation is one of the greatest arts in life— perhaps the greatest, and one cannot possibly learn it from anybody, that is the beauty of it. It has no technique and therefore no authority. When you learn about yourself, watch yourself, watch the way you walk, how you eat, what you say, the gossip, the hate, the jealousy—if you are aware of all that in yourself, without any choice, that is part of meditation.

So meditation can take place when you are sitting in a bus or walking in the woods full of light and shadows, or listening to the singing of birds or looking at the face of your wife or child.

In the understanding of meditation there is love, and love is not the product of systems, of habits, of following a method. Love cannot be cultivated by thought. Love can perhaps come into being when there is complete silence, a silence in which the meditator is entirely absent; and the mind can be silent only when it understands its own movement as thought and feeling. To understand this movement of thought and feeling there can be no condemnation in observing it. To observe in such a way is the discipline, and that kind of discipline is fluid, free, not the discipline of conformity.

学到，而这正是它的美。它没有技巧，因而也没有权威。当你了解自己，观察自己，观察你走路的样子、吃东西的样子，观察你说的话，观察流言、怨恨、嫉妒，如果你觉察到自己身上的那一切，却又毫无选择，这便是冥想的一部分。

因此，当你乘着巴士，或是漫步于光影斑驳的树林，或是聆听鸟儿的歌唱，又或是凝望着妻儿的脸庞，冥想都可能不期而至。

对冥想的了解当中就有着爱，而爱并非遵循体系、习惯以及方法的结果。爱无法由思想培植。当全然的寂静出现，冥想者在那寂静中完全缺席，爱或许方能到来。只有心懂得了自身思想和感受的全部活动，它才能安静下来。若要了解思想和感受的活动，观察当中便不能有一丝谴责。这样的观察便是纪律，这种纪律是流动的、自由的，而不是那种言听计从的纪律。

PART 16
第十六部分

Total Revolution—The Religious
Mind—Energy—Passion
彻底的革命——宗教之心——能
量——激情

What we have been concerned with all through this book is the bringing about in ourselves, and therefore in our lives, of a total revolution that has nothing whatsoever to do with the structure of society as it is. Society as it is, is a horrifying thing with its endless wars of aggression, whether that aggression be defensive or offensive. What we need is something totally new—a revolution, a mutation, in the psyche itself. The old brain cannot possibly solve the human problem of relationship. The old brain is Asiatic, European, American or African, so what we are asking ourselves is whether it is possible to bring about a mutation in the brain cells themselves?

Let us ask ourselves again, now that we have come to understand ourselves better, is it possible for a human being living an ordinary everyday life in this brutal, violent, ruthless world—a world which is becoming more and more efficient and therefore more and more ruthless - is it possible for him to bring about a revolution not only in his outward relationships but in the whole field of his thinking, feeling, acting and reacting.

Every day we see or read of appalling things happening in the world as the result of violence in man. You may say, "I can't do anything about it", or, "How can I influence the world?" I think you can tremendously influence the world if in yourself you are not violent, if you lead actually every day a peaceful life—a life which is not competitive, ambitious, envious—a life which does not create enmity. Small fires can become a blaze. We have reduced the world to its present state of chaos by our

贯穿这本书的始终，我们探讨的一直是在我们自己身上，进而在我们的生活中带来一场彻底的革命——这场革命与如今的社会结构没有半点关系。现今的社会非常可怕，有着永无止境的侵略战争，无论那种侵略是防卫型还是进攻型。我们需要的是某种崭新的东西——心智本身的一场革命，一种突变。旧大脑不可能解决人类的关系问题，旧大脑割裂成了亚洲、欧洲、美洲、非洲等各个视角，因此我们问自己：是否可能为脑细胞本身带来一场突变？

既然我们对自己已经有了更深入的了解，我们再来问问自己：在这个残酷、暴力、无情的世界上——这个世界正变得越来越高效，因而也变得越来越无情——一个过着日常生活的普通人，是否可能既为他的外部关系，也为他思考、感受、行动和反应的整个领域，带来一场革命？

我们每天都会见到或是读到世界上发生的那些可怕的事，那是人类内心暴力的结果。你也许会说："我对此无能为力"，或者："我怎么可能影响全世界呢？"可我认为，只要你自己不再暴力，只要你每天都真正过着一种和平的生活——一种没有竞争、野心、嫉妒的生活，一种不会制造敌意的生活——你便会对整个世界产生不可估量的影响，小小的火苗可以燃起烈焰。我们用自己自私的行为，用我们的

self-centred activity, by our prejudices, our hatreds, our nationalism, and when we say we cannot do anything about it, we are accepting disorder in ourselves as inevitable. We have splintered the world into fragments and if we ourselves are broken, fragmented, our relationship with the world will also be broken. But if, when we act, we act totally, then our relationship with the world undergoes a tremendous revolution.

After all, any movement which is worth while, any action which has any deep significance, must begin with each one of us. I must change first; I must see what is the nature and structure of my relationship with the world—and in the very seeing is the doing; therefore I, as a human being living in the world, bring about a different quality, and that quality, it seems to me, is the quality of the religious mind.

The religious mind is something entirely different from the mind that believes in religion. You cannot be religious and yet be a Hindu, a Muslim, a Christian, a Buddhist. A religious mind does not seek at all, it cannot experiment with truth. Truth is not something dictated by your pleasure or pain, or by your conditioning as a Hindu or whatever religion you belong to. The religious mind is a state of mind in which there is no fear and therefore no belief whatsoever but only what is—what actually is.

In the religious mind there is that state of silence we have already examined which is not produced by thought but is the outcome of awareness, which is meditation when the meditator is entirely absent. In that silence there is a state of energy in which there is no conflict. Energy is action and movement. All action is movement and all action is energy. All desire is energy. All feeling is energy. All thought is energy. All living is energy. All life is energy. If that energy is allowed to flow without any contradiction, without any friction, without any conflict, then that energy

偏见、我们的仇恨、我们的国家主义，把世界糟蹋成了如今的一片混乱。如果我们说自己对此无能为力，我们就接受了自身的混乱是在所难免的。我们把这个世界割裂成了碎片，如果我们自己都是破碎的、分裂的，我们与世界的关系也必然会破裂。但是，如果我们行动起来，如果我们的行动是完满的，那么我们与世界的关系便会发生一场巨大的革命。

毕竟，任何有价值的活动，任何意义深远的行动，都必须从我们每一个人开始。我自己必须首先转变，我必须看清自己与世界的关系具有怎样的本质与结构，"看见"本身之中便有行动。因此，身为活在世上的一个人，我将会带来一种截然不同的品质，而这份品质，在我看来，便是宗教之心的品质。

宗教之心与笃信宗教的心是截然不同的两码事。你不可能既具有宗教精神，同时又是一名印度教徒、穆斯林、基督教徒或是佛教徒。一颗宗教之心完全无所追寻，它不会把真理当作实验品。真理绝不会受制于你的苦与乐，也不会受制于你身为印度教徒或是无论什么教徒所受的局限。宗教之心即是这样一种心灵状态：无所畏惧，因而没有任何信仰，而只有"现实"——当下真切的事实。

宗教之心具备我们之前所探讨的那种寂静状态，那份寂静并非思想所造，而是源于觉察，也就是冥想者完全缺席的冥想。那份寂静中有一种毫无冲突的能量，而能量便是行动和运动。一切行动都是运动，一切行动也都是能量。所有欲望、所有感受、所有思想都是能量，所有生活、所有生命也都是能量。如果允许能量毫无矛盾、毫无

is boundless, endless. When there is no friction there are no frontiers to energy. It is friction which gives energy limitations. So, having once seen this, why is it that the human being always brings friction into energy? Why does he create friction in this movement which we call life? Is pure energy, energy without limitation, just an idea to him? Does it have no reality?

We need energy not only to bring about a total revolution in ourselves but also in order to investigate, to look, to act. And as long as there is friction of any kind in any of our relationships, whether between husband and wife, between man and man, between one community and another or one country and another or one ideology and another—if there is any inward friction or any outward conflict in any form, however subtle it may be—there is a waste of energy.

As long as there is a time interval between the observer and the observed it creates friction and therefore there is a waste of energy. That energy is gathered to its highest point when the observer is the observed, in which there is no time interval at all. Then there will be energy without motive and it will find its own channel of action because then the "I" does not exist.

We need a tremendous amount of energy to understand the confusion in which we live, and the feeling, "I must understand", brings about the vitality to find out. But finding out, searching, implies time, and, as we have seen, gradually to uncondition the mind is not the way. Time is not the way. Whether we are old or young it is now that the whole process of life can be brought into a different dimension. Seeking the opposite of what we are is not the way either, nor is the artificial discipline imposed by a system, a teacher, a philosopher or priest—all that is so very childish. When we realize this, we ask ourselves is it possible to break through this heavy conditioning of centuries immediately and not enter into another conditioning—to be free, so that the

摩擦、毫无冲突地流动，能量便是无界的、无限的。只要没有摩擦，能量便没有疆界，正是摩擦局限了能量。那么，既然曾经看到过这一点，为什么人类还总是让能量有摩擦呢？他为什么要在我们叫作"生活"的运动中制造摩擦？纯粹的能量，无限的能量，对他来说只是个概念吗？它没有任何真实性吗？

不仅带来我们自身的彻底革命需要能量，探究、观察、行动也需要能量。而只要我们的任何关系中存在任何一种摩擦——无论是夫妻关系，个人之间、社团之间、国家之间还是意识形态之间的关系——只要存在任何形式的内在摩擦或是外在冲突，无论多么细微，都会造成能量的浪费。

只要观察者与被观察者之间存在时间隔阂，就会制造摩擦，进而造成能量的浪费。而当观察者与被观察者合而为一，不存在任何时间隔阂，能量便会积聚到最高点。此时便会有毫无动机的能量，它会找到自己行动的渠道，因为那时"我"已不复存在。

我们需要惊人的能量来了解我们所处的混乱，这份"我必须了解"的感受，便带来了探明真相的活力。但探究、寻求当中隐含着时间，正如我们所发现的那样，逐步解除心灵的制约并非出路，时间并非出路。无论我们老迈还是年轻，只能当下一刻便把生命的整个过程带入一个迥异的维度。追求我们现状的对立面不是出路，由体系、导师、哲学家或是牧师所强加的人为戒律也不是出路——那一切都太幼稚了。当我们认识到这一点，我们问自己：有没有可能即刻打破几百年来的沉重制约，同时又不落入另一种束缚——有没有可能获得彻底

mind can be altogether new, sensitive, alive, aware, intense, capable? That is our problem. There is no other problem because when the mind is made new it can tackle any problem. That is the only question we have to ask ourselves.

But we do not ask. We want to be told. One of the most curious things in the structure of our psyche is that we all want to be told because we are the result of the propaganda of ten thousand years. We want to have our thinking confirmed and corroborated by another, whereas to ask a question is to ask it of yourself. What I say has very little value. You will forget it the moment you shut this book, or you will remember and repeat certain phrases, or you will compare what you have read here with some other book - but you will not face your own life. And that is all that matters—your life, yourself, your pettiness, your shallowness, your brutality, your violence, your greed, your ambition, your daily agony and endless sorrow—that is what you have to understand and nobody on earth or in heaven is going to save you from it but yourself.

Seeing everything that goes on in your daily life, your daily activities - when you pick up a pen, when you talk, when you go out for a drive or when you are walking alone in the woods—can you with one breath, with one look, know yourself very simply as you are? When you know yourself as you are, then you understand the whole structure of man's endeavour, his deceptions, his hypocrisies, his search. To do this you must be tremendously honest with yourself throughout your being. When you act according to your principles you are being dishonest because when you act according to what you think you ought to be you are not what you are. It is a brutal thing to have ideals. If you have any ideals, beliefs or principles you cannot possibly look at yourself directly. So can you be completely negative, completely quiet, neither thinking nor afraid, and yet be extraordinarily, passionately alive?

的自由，于是心能够变得崭新、敏感、鲜活、觉知、热情、能干？这便是我们的问题，没有其他的问题，因为只要心焕然一新，它便可以解决任何问题。这便是我们唯一要问自己的问题。

但我们从不问自己，我们希望别人来告诉我们。我们心智结构中最奇怪的一件事，便是我们都希望听命于他人，因为我们是上万年来洗脑的产物。我们希望自己的想法得到别人的肯定与支持，但提出一个问题，实际上是要问问你自己。我所说的话没什么价值，你一合上书便会忘掉，或者你会记得并重复某些只言片语，又或者你会把读到的内容与另一些书籍做比较，但你不会面对自己的生活。但那才是唯一重要的事——你的生活，你自己，你的卑微，你的肤浅，你的残忍，你的暴力，你的贪婪，你的野心，你每天的痛苦和无尽的悲伤——那才是你必须了解的。然而，即使上天入地都没有哪个人能把你从中拯救出来，除了你自己。

看到了你日常生活中所发生的一切、你的日常行为——当你捡起一支笔，当你开口说话，当你开车出门兜风，或是当你独自在林中漫步——你能否在呼吸之间、在一瞥之中便简简单单地、如实地认清自己？当你如实地认清了自己，你便能了解人类费力奋争的整个结构——他的自欺，他的虚伪，他的追寻。要做到这一点，你就必须全身心地对自己保持高度的诚实。当你按照自己的原则去行动，你就是不诚实的，因为当你按自认为应当的样子去行动，你便不再是真实的自己了。心怀理想是一件残忍的事，只要你抱有任何理想、信仰或是原则，你便无法直接看清自己。那么，你能否彻底否定、彻底安

That state of mind which is no longer capable of striving is the true religious mind, and in that state of mind you may come upon this thing called truth or reality or bliss or God or beauty or love. This thing cannot be invited. Please understand that very simple fact. It cannot be invited, it cannot be sought after, because the mind is too silly, too small, your emotions are too shoddy, your way of life too confused for that enormity, that immense something, to be invited into your little house, your little corner of living which has been trampled and spat upon. You cannot invite it. To invite it you must know it and you cannot know it. It doesn't matter who says it, the moment he says, "I know", he does not know. The moment you say you have found it you have not found it. If you say you have experienced it, you have never experienced it. Those are all ways of exploiting another man—your friend or your enemy.

One asks oneself then whether it is possible to come upon this thing without inviting, without waiting, without seeking or exploring—just for it to happen like a cool breeze that comes in when you leave the window open? You cannot invite the wind but you must leave the window open, which doesn't mean that you are in a state of waiting; that is another form of deception. It doesn't mean you must open yourself to receive; that is another kind of thought.

Haven't you ever asked yourself why it is that human beings lack this thing? They beget children, they have sex, tenderness, a quality of sharing something together in companionship, in friendship, in fellowship, but this thing—why is it they haven't got it? Haven't you ever wondered lazily on occasion when you are walking by yourself in a filthy street or sitting in a bus or are on holiday by the seaside or walking in a wood with a lot of birds, trees, streams and wild animals—hasn't it ever come upon you to ask

静，既不思考也不害怕，同时又激情四射、生机勃勃？

不再费力奋争的心灵状态即是真正的宗教之心，在那种心灵状态之下，你也许便会邂逅这件被称为真理、真相、极乐、神、美或是爱的事物。但你无法邀约它，请理解这个非常简单的事实。它无法邀请，无法寻获，因为心智太过愚蠢、太过狭隘，你的情感太过卑微，你的生活方式太过混乱，完全无法邀约那浩瀚无垠的事物进入你那狭小的房间，你那惨遭践踏和践踏的生活角落。你无法邀约它。若想邀请它，你就必须认得它，但你无法认识它。无论是谁，一旦他说"我知道"，他实际上并不知道。一旦你说你已经找到了它，你实际上并非找到。如果你说你体验到了它，你实际上从未体验过。这些都是剥削他人——剥削你的朋友或是敌人的手段。

此时你便会问自己：有没有可能邂逅这样东西，无须邀约，无须等待，也无须追寻或是探求——只是让它自然发生，就像你开窗迎来的一阵清风？你无法邀约清风进来，但你必须打开窗子。但这并不是说你处于等待状态，那是另一种形式的自欺；也不是说你必须打开自己去接受什么，那不过是另一种理念罢了。

你难道不曾问过自己，为什么人类缺少这样东西？他们生儿育女，他们享有性爱与温存，伴侣、朋友关系之中也有一种同甘共苦的品质，但这样东西他们为什么偏偏没有？当你独自走在肮脏的街道上，当你乘着巴士，当你在海边度假，或是走在林中，周围环绕着数不清的鸟儿、树木、溪流和野生动物，你难道就不曾偶尔懒懒地感到好奇，问一问为什么人类生活了数百万年，却依然没有这样东西，这

why it is that man, who has lived for millions and millions of years, has not got this thing, this extraordinary unfading flower? Why is it that you, as a human being, who are so capable, so clever, so cunning, so competitive, who have such marvellous technology, who go to the skies and under the earth and beneath the sea, and invent extraordinary electronic brains— why is it that you haven't got this one thing which matters? I don't know whether you have ever seriously faced this issue of why your heart is empty.

What would your answer be if you put the question to yourself—your direct answer without any equivocation or cunningness? Your answer would be in accordance with your intensity in asking the question and the urgency of it. But you are neither intense nor urgent, and that is because you haven't got energy, energy being passion—and you cannot find any truth without passion—passion with a fury behind it, passion in which there is no hidden want. Passion is a rather frightening thing because if you have passion you don't know where it will take you.

So is fear perhaps the reason why you have not got the energy of that passion to find out for yourself why this quality of love is missing in you, why there is not this flame in your heart? If you have examined your own mind and heart very closely, you will know why you haven't got it. If you are passionate in your discovery to find why you haven't got it, you will know it is there. Through complete negation alone, which is the highest form of passion, that thing which is love, comes into being. Like humility you cannot cultivate love. Humility comes into being when there is a total ending of conceit—then you will never know what it is to be humble. A man who knows what it is to have humility is a vain man. In the same way when you give your mind and your heart, your nerves, your eyes, your whole being to find out the way of life, to see what actually is and go

朵永不凋零的奇葩？你，身为人类的一员，如此聪明能干，如此机灵狡黠，如此富有竞争力，掌握了如此非凡的科技，上天入地下海无所不能，还发明了不可思议的电脑，可你为什么还是没有这一样最重要的东西？我不知道你可曾认真地面对这个问题：你的心为何如此空洞？

如果你问自己这个问题，你会如何作答——你毫不含糊也毫不狡黠的直接答复会是什么？你的回答取决于你提问的热切度与紧迫度。但你既不热切也不紧迫，那就是你为什么没有能量即激情的原因——而没有激情你无法找到任何真相。激情背后藏有烈焰，激情之中没有隐藏的欲求。激情是一样相当可怕的东西，因为如果你有了激情，你完全不知道它将会把你带到哪里。

那么，有没有可能是因为恐惧，让你没有那股激情的能量，去亲自发现为什么你身上缺少那份爱的品质，为什么你内心没有那团火焰？如果你非常密切地审视过自己的头脑和内心，你就会明白你为什么没有它了。如果你满怀激情地去探索你为什么没有它，你便会发现它已经在那里了。经由彻底的否定——那是最高形式的激情——那样东西，也就是爱，便出现了。爱像谦卑一样无法培养。当自负彻底终结，谦卑便会出现，但此时你绝不会知道何为谦卑。一个知道如何拥有谦卑的人，便是一个自负的人。同样，当你付出你的头脑、你的心、你的神经、你的眼睛，付出你的整个存在去探究生活之道，看清当下的事实并超越它，全然地、彻底地否定你如今的生活方式，在对丑陋、残忍的否定当中，另一样东西便出现了。而你也

beyond it, and deny completely, totally, the life you live now - in that very denial of the ugly, the brutal, the other comes into being. And you will never know it either. A man who knows that he is silent, who knows that he loves, does not know what love is or what silence is.

绝不会认出它。一个自认为寂静，自认为有爱的人，并不知道何为

爱，何为寂静。

.